250

*A*pproaching

*Z*anzibar

and

Other Plays

Approaching Zanzibar

and

Other Plays

TINA HOWE

Theatre Communications Group

Approaching Zanzibar and Other Plays is published by Theatre Communications Group, Inc., 355 Lexington Ave., New York, NY 10017-0217.

Howe, Tina.
    Approaching Zanzibar and other plays / Tina Howe. —1st ed.
    Contents: Approaching Zanzibar—Birth and after birth—One shoe off.
              ISBN 1-55936-104-2
                    I. Title.
          PS3558.0894A86   1995
    812'.54—dc20   94-44575
                                   CIP

Cover: Christo and Jeanne-Claude: "Running Fence, Sonoma and Marin Counties, California, 1972–76," Copyright © 1976 by Christo
The author wishes to thank Christo and Jeanne-Claude for their largesse in sharing this photograph.

Photograph by Wolfgang Volz
Typeset by The Typeworks

To the memory of
Richard Jordan
1937–1993

Contents

Introduction

These are the plays that got me into trouble. No one would produce *Birth and After Birth* after it was written; *Approaching Zanzibar* left many critics mystified and *One Shoe Off* received universally hostile reviews. What do these works have in common and why did they cause such distress?

They're about the dailiness of women's lives—marriage, child raising, housekeeping and entertaining—subjects that many consider unworthy of the stage. To make matters worse, they're written on a dizzy operatic scale. When a four-year-old celebrates his birthday, he dresses up in his mother's underwear; when a menopausal woman gets hot flashes, she rips off her blouse; and when a salad is tossed at a dinner party, it's flung all over the guests.

Having come of age during the heyday of the Absurdists, I always felt theatre should shake up our perceptions so we can see life through fresh eyes. My models were Pirandello, Genet, Ionesco, Beckett and Albee. I delighted in how they scrambled relationships, gender, setting and language, whipping up plays that were haunting, hilarious and profound. "Yes, yes!" I cried. "This is the style for me."

I plunged into *Birth and After Birth* in 1970, eager to explore the wonder and terror of motherhood. Three years later I emerged with an opéra bouffe in which couples spar over their fertility, a false birth is reenacted onstage and a large hairy man plays a four-year-old. Needless to say, every self-respecting theatre in the country turned it down. The Absurdists can shake up our preconceptions about power and identity, but for a woman to take on the sanctity of motherhood . . . Even my agent at the time dismissed me.

So I turned to less threatening arenas—museums, restaurants, Beacon Hill drawing rooms and New England beaches. These plays fared much better. I won awards, was heralded in the *New York Times* and appeared on panels with the major playwrights of the day. I was inching towards fifty and starting to feel my mortality. I was desperate to give voice to this crisis from a female perspective, but would I survive the attempt?

As always, I embraced the Absurdists as models, playing loose with language and event. *Approaching Zanzibar* was the result. The women in the audience were rhapsodic, the men, divided. After years of being viewed as a well-heeled WASPy playwright, I suddenly emerged as a feminist. My early fans of *Birth and After Birth* already knew about these stirrings, but now it was out in the open. Menopausal women heard babies crying in the bushes; dying old ladies recalled forbidden love affairs; and ten-year-old girls ate flowers to stem their fear of death.

It's one thing for male playwrights to show women overwrought with passion and self-loathing—when women do it, the rhythms and details are different. Ambiguity rushes in and therein lies the threat. We tend to see conflicting aspects of a situation at the same time, blending the tragic, comic, noble and absurd. It's something women poets and novelists have been doing for years. Women playwrights have to walk a finer line. We can entertain, but the minute we step into deeper water, beware . . .

It's a happy coincidence of fate that these plays are being published together. The careful reader will recognize *One Shoe Off* as a continuation of *Birth and After Birth*. *One Shoe Off*'s Dinah and Leonard are the Apples of *Birth and After Birth* twenty years later. Nicky has grown up and left home. It's just the two of them now; the battle lines are more sharply drawn. They're still preparing for a party, but now the fate of their marriage rests on the outcome. The first play's sea images have been replaced with a vegetable riot, and the house is now literally sinking into the ground. It's complicated stuff that calls for surrender, and surrender is at the heart of appreciating women's writing. We don't get from A to Z in a straight line. We set up roadblocks and detours to enliven the journey because, as the poet says, "The impeded spring is the one that sings."

Tina Howe
New York City
December 1994

Characters

WALLACE BLOSSOM, a composer, 49
CHARLOTTE BLOSSOM, his wife, 45
TURNER BLOSSOM, their son, a prodigy, 12
PONY BLOSSOM, their nearsighted daughter, 9
RANDY WANDS, a new father, 43
PALACE ST. JOHN, a hearty grandmother, 63
FLETCHER ST. JOHN, her deaf grandson, 11
SCOTTY CHILDS, Charlotte's brother, a landscape architect, 48
JOY CHILDS, his new wife, an African-American TV newscaster
  who's seven months pregnant, 28
AMY CHILDS, Scotty's athletic daughter, played by a boy, 11
DALIA PAZ, Olivia's Mexican nurse, 28
OLIVIA CHILDS, Charlotte's aunt, an eminent site-specific
  artist, 81
DR. SYBIL WREN, her doctor, with a severe limp, 60s

Approaching Zanzibar was originally produced by the Second
Stage Theatre, New York City, Carole Rothman and Robyn
Goodman, Artistic Directors.

Act One

SCENE 1

The Blossoms are driving towards Falling Waters, West Virginia, in a station wagon. It's the first week of August, around ten in the evening. Wally's at the wheel and Charlotte sits next to him. Turner and Pony are piled in the back along with all their gear. Pony wears glasses. They're all singing "Ninety-nine Bottles of Beer on the Wall" with flagging energy.

ALL:
Forty-four bottles of beer on the wall,
Forty-four bottles of beer,
If one of those bottles should happen to fall,
Forty-three bottles of beer on the wall.

Forty-three bottles of beer on the wall,
Forty-three bottles of beer,
If one of those bottles should happen to fall,
Forty-two bottles of beer on the wall.

Forty-two bottles of beer on the wall,
Forty-two bottles of beer,
If one of those bottles should happen to fall,
Forty-one bottles of beer on the wall . . .
CHARLOTTE: STOP . . . STOP . . . I CAN'T TAKE IT ANYMORE!

3

WALLY, TURNER AND PONY:
    Forty-one bottles of beer on the wall,
    Forty-one bottles of beer,
    If one of those bottles should happen to fall,
    Forty bottles of beer on the wall.
CHARLOTTE: Pleeeease?
TURNER AND PONY (*Softly*):
    Forty bottles of beer on the wall,
    Forty bottles of beer,
    If one of those bottles should happen to fall . . .
WALLY: Your mother asked you to stop.
TURNER AND PONY (*Softer*):
    Thirty-nine bottles of beer on the wall.
    Thirty-nine bottles of beer on the wall,
    Thirty-nine bottles of beer,
    If one of those bottles should happen to fall . . .
CHARLOTTE: Kids . . . ?!
TURNER AND PONY (*Barely audible*):
    Thirty-eight bottles of beer on the wall . . .
WALLY: IF YOU DON'T STOP RIGHT THIS MINUTE,
    I'M PULLING OVER TO THE SIDE OF THE ROAD!

They keep humming. The sound of screeching brakes as Wally veers over to the side of the road. They all lean to the right.

CHARLOTTE: LOOK OUT, LOOK OUT!	TURNER AND PONY: We stopped, we stopped!

A silence. Wally straightens the wheel and eases back onto the road.

WALLY: Thank you.

Charlotte sighs deeply. Silence as Wally drives.

PONY: Are we there yet?
WALLY: We just started, for Christsakes! We have two thousand
    more miles to go!

CHARLOTTE: Why do they always have to push us to the breaking point? Why . . . ? It's not fair.

Pause.

WALLY *(Suddenly whirls around, glaring at the kids)*: Answer her! WHY DO YOU ALWAYS HAVE TO PUSH US TO THE BREAKING POINT, HUH . . . ? HUH . . . ?!

PONY: I didn't do anything.

TURNER: Don't look at me. Pony was the one who—

CHARLOTTE: WALLY, EYES ON THE ROAD, PLEASE!

PONY: Right, right, it's always *my* fault.

WALLY *(Turning back towards the road)*: Sorry, sorry . . .

TURNER *(To Pony)*: You were the one who kept singing.

PONY: You were singing too.

CHARLOTTE *(To Wally)*: You're already breaking the speed limit as it is.

TURNER *(To Pony)*: That's not true.

WALLY *(To Charlotte)*: Are you complaining about the way I'm driving?

TURNER *(To Pony)*: I stopped when Dad asked me to.

PONY: You did not!

TURNER: I did so!

PONY: Did not!

TURNER: Did so!

WALLY *(To Charlotte)*: Hello . . . ?

PONY: Did not!

Faster and faster.

TURNER: Did so!

PONY: Did not!

TURNER: Did so!

CHARLOTTE *(To Wally)*: I just wish you wouldn't go so fast.

PONY: Did not, did not, did NOT!

WALLY: Since when is sixty-five fast?

TURNER *(Shoving Pony)*: DID SO!

PONY: OW . . . OW . . . TURNER PUSHED ME!

CHARLOTTE: The speed limit is fifty-five.

WALLY: Would you like to drive?

Pony bites Turner's arm.

TURNER *(Leaping out of his seat)*: YIIIIII! PONY BIT ME!

CHARLOTTE: All I said was: you're breaking the speed limit. *(Turning around)* KIDS, PLEASE . . . ?!

WALLY: I happen to be a safe driver.

Turner gives Pony a noogie.

PONY *(Leaping out of her seat)*: OW, OW . . . TURNER GAVE ME A NOOGIE, TURNER GAVE ME A NOOGIE!

They start wrestling.

PONY: I'm going to get you, Turner. Hold still! Will you hold still? Turrrner . . . ?!	TURNER: Oh . . . so you want to fight do you . . . ? All right, Pony . . . say your prayers!

The wrestling gets more ferocious.

CHARLOTTE *(Whirling around)*: KIDS, WE ASKED YOU TO BEHAVE!

WALLY *(Also whirling around)*: ALL RIGHT, WHAT'S GOING ON BACK THERE?

CHARLOTTE *(Grabbing the wheel)*: LOOK OUT, LOOK OUT!

They all veer to one side as the tires squeal.

WALLY *(Grabbing it back)*: GIVE ME THAT WHEEL!

They veer to the other side.

CHARLOTTE: WALLY, WE ALMOST WENT OFF THE ROAD!

The kids keep slugging each other.

WALLY: JESUS CHRIST, CHARLOTTE...
CHARLOTTE: What are you trying to do...? *Kill* us?
WALLY: ...YOU DON'T GRAB THE STEERING WHEEL OUT OF SOMEONE'S HANDS!
CHARLOTTE: We were going off the road!

PONY: I hate you, I hate you, I hate you, I hate you, I hate you, I hate you, I hate you—	TURNER: If you hurt my hands, I'll smash you. I really mean it, I'll smash you!

Wally pulls over to the side of the road and slams on the brakes. Everyone lurches forward and then back.

CHARLOTTE: Wally, what are you...?
WALLY: *All right, that's it! That's it!*

A horrible silence.

WALLY *(Calm and collected)*: I can take a hint. If you don't like the way I'm driving, *you* drive! *(He gets out of the car, slams his door and marches over to the passenger side)*
CHARLOTTE: Wally...?!

He opens the door and pushes Charlotte over.

CHARLOTTE: Wally, what are you...?
WALLY: Come on, move over, move over!
CHARLOTTE: *Wallace...?!*
WALLY: I said...MOVE! *(He slams the door closed)*
CHARLOTTE: I didn't say I wanted to drive.
WALLY: Well, someone's got to drive if we want to make it to Rushing Rivers or wherever the hell it is...

CHARLOTTE: Hey, hey, *you* were the one who took the wrong turn off 81 . . .

WALLY: So now that's my fault too.

CHARLOTTE: And it's not Rushing Rivers, it's *Falling Waters*!

WALLY: Why we had to stop at Hershey, Pennsylvania, I'll never understand.

CHARLOTTE: Come on, you loved every minute of it!

WALLY: At the rate we're going, the campsite will be filled and we'll have to stay in a motel.

CHARLOTTE: Who had to go back in line a second time to watch the Chocolate Kisses being poured and wrapped, hmmmm?

WALLY: It's so typical. Our first day on the road and we'll have to stay in a motel! Pay a hundred and fifty bucks to sleep in some gummy room with a broken air conditioner . . . !

CHARLOTTE: We won't have to stay in a motel.

WALLY: If you'd been looking at the map instead of the god-damned speedometer all the time, I wouldn't have taken that turn!

CHARLOTTE: Okay, okay . . .

Pause.

CHARLOTTE: I just hate it when you speed. Especially with the kids in the car. It's just asking for trouble!

WALLY: I don't believe we're doing this. . . . *Driving* to New Mexico. How did you ever talk me into it?

Pause.

CHARLOTTE: If I hadn't grabbed the wheel, we'd all be lying dead in a ditch!

WALLY: Do you know how many more states we have to go through . . . ?

Pause.

CHARLOTTE: Is that how you want to start our vacation? All being piled into body bags at the side of the road?

WALLY: . . . Virginia, North Carolina, Tennessee, Alabama . . .

CHARLOTTE: We're not going anywhere *near* Alabama!

WALLY: Kentucky, Missouri, Arkansas, Oklahoma . . .

CHARLOTTE: She's dying, honey.

WALLY: There are about a hundred and fifty states between New York and New Mexico.

CHARLOTTE: I want to say goodbye.

WALLY: The airplane was invented for a reason, you know.

PONY: Mommy . . . ?

WALLY: Texas alone is the size of China.

CHARLOTTE: But I don't fly.

WALLY: Why do you have to take it out on us?

CHARLOTTE: Turner's never played for her. I want her to hear him.

PONY: Mommy . . . ?

WALLY: It'll take us seventy-five years to get there.

CHARLOTTE *(Opening her window)*: God, it's hot in here!

WALLY: We'll all be in walkers!

CHARLOTTE: Who's always complaining that we never take a vacation?

PONY: *Mommy . . . ?*

WALLY *(Putting on a creaky old voice)*: "Well, hi there Livvie, we finally made it! That *is* you, isn't it Liv? I don't see so good anymore."

PONY: Mommy, what's Livvie dying of?

TURNER: God Pony . . . !

WALLY *(Still playing aged)*: "Hey there, Char, want to pass me my ear trumpet? I don't hear so good neither."

CHARLOTTE: We'll finally get to see the country . . . swim in freshwater streams, camp out under the stars . . . *go fly-fishing*!

WALLY: Well, at least I convinced you to leave Spit and Wheat Germ behind in a kennel.

PONY: Oh Spit . . . !

TURNER: Spitty, Spitty, Spit!

PONY: I MISS SPIT!

CHARLOTTE: We're going to have a great time! I can feel it!

PONY: I MISS SPIT, I	TURNER: SPITTY,
MISS SPIT, I MISS	SPITTY SPIT! SPITTY,
SPIT, I MISS SPIT, I	SPITTY SPIT! SPITTY,
MISS SPIT . . . !	SPITTY SPIT . . . !

They start barking.

CHARLOTTE: We'll get to spend some time with Scotty and
Joy. We haven't seen them since the wedding. *(Turning around)*
Remember Joy, kids?

WALLY: She is one classy lady. I don't know how Scotty ever
nabbed her.

CHARLOTTE *(To the kids)*: Come on, quiet down.

WALLY *(As a rallying cry)*: We'll get to see Amy again!

CHARLOTTE *(Groaning)*: Please!

*Pony and Turner are now baying, yelping, panting and making
other assorted canine sounds.*

CHARLOTTE *(Whirling*	WALLY *(Likewise)*: JESUS
around): KIDS, PLEASE!	CHRIST GUYS, WILL
DADDY AND I ARE	YOU PIPE DOWN?
TRYING TO HAVE A	THIS ISN'T A
CONVERSATION!	KENNEL!

Silence.

CHARLOTTE: God . . . !

WALLY: Give us a break!

CHARLOTTE: I mean, after a while . . .

Silence.

PONY *(In a tiny voice)*: Mommy . . . ?

WALLY: There *are* other people in the car, you know.

CHARLOTTE: Daddy and I have *some* rights . . .

Silence.

WALLY *(To Charlotte)*: So, are we going to sit here all night, or what?

PONY: Mommy . . . ?

CHARLOTTE: Oh right, right. Sorry. *(She swings back onto the road)*

TURNER: Where are we, anyway?

PONY: Mommy . . . ?

WALLY: *Who knows!*

PONY: I have to pee.

TURNER: You just went fifteen minutes ago.

CHARLOTTE: Why didn't you say something when we were stopped? *(Opening her window wider)* God, I'm burning up!

WALLY: So guys, is everyone ready for . . . *(Trumpet-fanfare sound)* Gamey Amy?!

CHARLOTTE:	TURNER: Spare	PONY: She's so
(Laughing):	me!	weird . . . !
Oh no!		

WALLY: Boy wonder of the western world!

CHARLOTTE *(Trying not to laugh)*: Come on, don't be mean.

PONY: Mommy . . . ?

WALLY: The only eight-year-old girl I know who can throw a shot put fifty yards.

CHARLOTTE: Honey, she's eleven!

WALLY: And already shaving! *(He mimes using an electric razor)*

PONY: Mommy?

Turner joins Wally shaving.

CHARLOTTE *(Trying not to laugh)*: Come on, guys!

PONY: I have to pee, I have to pee!

WALLY: Charlotte, the girl's got sideburns and a moustache!

PONY: EWWWWWW! TURNER: Gross, gross!

CHARLOTTE: She's just very athletic. Look at her mother.

WALLY: That's a marriage I'll never understand. Your brother and Inge Trim . . .

CHARLOTTE: She was blonde, Swedish and a world-class track star.

TURNER: How many Olympic medals has she won?

WALLY: About three hundred. The woman lives to compete. I've never seen anything like it. *(To the kids)* She had Amy running a four-minute mile by the time she was seven.

CHARLOTTE: Honey . . . ?!

WALLY: And remember that craze with pole vaulting? Amy would start tearing up the driveway with this special broomstick and then BOIIIIIINGGGGG . . . she'd suddenly be flying over the family car!

CHARLOTTE: *Wally . . . ?!*

WALLY: Inge Trim. . . . She had calves like a weightlifter.

PONY: I like Joy better.

CHARLOTTE: We all like Joy better. Scotty should have married her in the first place.

PONY: She's so beautiful.

CHARLOTTE: And *kind* . . . !

WALLY: She's also the first black newscaster in Oklahoma City, which is no small feat.

CHARLOTTE: She's wonderful. Amy adores her.

WALLY: Poor Amy.

CHARLOTTE: Poor Amy!

WALLY: Where was it she just won that big hang-gliding contest . . . ? Colorado? Wyoming? Arizona? No, wait, I remember, it was in Salt Lake City.

TURNER: Hey, let's play Geography again!

PONY *(Clapping her hands)*: Geography, Geography, Geography!

CHARLOTTE: Oh, not again!

WALLY: Great idea!

PONY AND TURNER: Geography, Geography, Geography!

WALLY: Alabama!

TURNER: Arkansas! That ends in S, Pone.

PONY: I know, I know. . . . South Dakota!

TURNER: Mom . . . ?

WALLY: It's your turn, Char.

CHARLOTTE (*Opening her window more*): Sorry, sorry, I need more air.

TURNER: We're waiting . . .

CHARLOTTE (*Fanning herself as she drives*): Okay, okay . . . what did you say?

WALLY, TURNER AND PONY: SOUTH DAKOTA!

CHARLOTTE (*Recoils from the blast*): Arizona!

WALLY: Annapolis!

TURNER: Salem!

PONY: Mississippi!

WALLY: Islip!

TURNER: Islip? Where's Islip?

WALLY AND CHARLOTTE: Long Island.

WALLY: Go on Turner. You start with P.

TURNER: Um . . . Princeton!

Faster and faster.

PONY: New Mexico!

CHARLOTTE: Ohio!

WALLY: Oklahoma!

TURNER: Atlanta!

PONY: Alabama!

TURNER: Daddy already said Alabama. You're out, you're out.

WALLY AND CHARLOTTE: You're out, you're out!

PONY: No fair, no fair!

TURNER: Pony's out.

WALLY AND CHARLOTTE (*With an edge*): Pony's out, Pony's out!

PONY (*Near tears*): No fair, I'm always out first. It's not fair.

SCENE 2

Luray, Virginia, two days and 134 miles later. It's eight in the morning and pouring rain. The Blossoms are huddled around the door of their tent in their pajamas, glumly staring out.

WALLY: Well, there goes our hike up White Oak Canyon Trail.

CHARLOTTE: Just our luck!

PONY *(Yelling out at it)*: LOUSY STINKY RAIN!

TURNER *(Leaning out the door, with his hands out, impressed)*: Whoa, look at it come down!

CHARLOTTE *(Pulling Turner back in)*: Get back in here, you'll get soaked!

WALLY: Well, at least it stopped thundering and lightning.

A great crash of thunder and lightning shivers around them.

PONY: HELP . . .   TURNER: FAR OUT!
HELP . . . !

CHARLOTTE *(Terrified, drags them away from the door)*: LOOK OUT, LOOK OUT!

WALLY: Me and my big mouth!

CHARLOTTE *(Drops to the floor with her arms over her head)*: Quick, down on the floor.

TURNER: Mom . . . ?

WALLY: Take it easy, Charlotte.

CHARLOTTE *(Rocking back and forth)*: Our Father who art in Heaven, hallowed be thy name. Thy kingdom come, thy will be done on earth as it is in Heaven. Give us this day our daily bread . . .

TURNER: It was just a little thunder.

PONY *(Suddenly all smiles)*: That was neat!

They stare at Charlotte as she continues to pray.

WALLY *(Goes over to Charlotte, offering her his hand)*: Honey . . . ?

CHARLOTTE *(Being pulled to her feet)*: Sorry, sorry. You know me and thunderstorms . . .

TURNER: Did you know that fireflies are immune to lightning? It just bounces right off them.

WALLY: Where did you hear that?

TURNER: Salvatore Argenti told me.

CHARLOTTE: God, it looks as if a bomb went off in here!

WALLY: Salvatore Argenti . . . ?

CHARLOTTE: Come on guys, what do you say we start straightening up? *(She begins folding a brightly woven blanket)*

TURNER: He told me during our master class last month.

CHARLOTTE: Wal, want to give me a hand with this?

WALLY: He did? Where was I? *(He helps Charlotte fold)* This is really beautiful. You know you're a damned good weaver.

CHARLOTTE: Why, thank you.

WALLY: I wish you'd take it more seriously.

CHARLOTTE: Honey, I don't have time anymore what with the kids . . .

TURNER: He said that because they're already filled with light, they can never be hurt by it. It's the same with electric eels . . .

CHARLOTTE *(Voice lowered)*: He was using it as a metaphor about prodigies.

WALLY: Right, right, I remember.

TURNER: They can't be electrocuted.

Pony runs to a corner of the tent and stands on her head.

CHARLOTTE: Too much talent never destroyed anyone.

PONY: HEY, EVERYBODY LOOK AT ME!

TURNER: Pony, one of these days your brains are going to fall out. They're just going to start oozing out your ears.

WALLY *(Starts folding a sleeping bag)*: It's the goddamned world that mucks everything up. You're plodding along writing your trios and suites and . . . FOOM . . .

TURNER: Blub, blub, blub . . . *(Etc.)*

WALLY: . . . suddenly the melodies elude you.

PONY: It's so neat seeing everything upside down.

WALLY: A great silence descends . . .

CHARLOTTE *(Also folding a bag)*: Careful Pony, or you'll break your glasses again. Come on kids, pitch in.

WALLY: Thank God for teaching.

PONY: Your mouths look so funny when you talk . . . *(She exaggerates her jaw movements)* Ba ba ba ba ba ba ba . . . *(Etc.)*

WALLY *(Moving on to the kids' sleeping bags)*: So . . . how did everybody sleep last night?

CHARLOTTE: Don't ask. *(Mopping her brow)* God, it's hot in here!

PONY: You look like marionettes. . . . Ba ba ba ba ba . . .

CHARLOTTE *(To Wally)*: I heard the baby again.

WALLY: Honey, it's just a dream.

PONY: Come on Turn, join me. It's so fun. Ba ba ba ba . . .

TURNER: Yeah . . . ? *(He stands on his head next to her)*

CHARLOTTE: Wally, I heard it!

WALLY: People don't abandon babies in the wilderness. They leave them in bus terminals or movie theaters.

CHARLOTTE: It was sobbing and sobbing as if its little heart would break.

TURNER: This *is* neat! *(Imitating them)* Ba ba ba ba ba . . .

CHARLOTTE: I almost went out to look for him.

WALLY: Him? How do you know it's a boy?

CHARLOTTE: Because I saw him.

WALLY: You *saw* him? When did you see him?

CHARLOTTE: The night before last.

WALLY: But we were in West Virginia.

Turner and Pony flop back down to their feet to listen.

CHARLOTTE: It's weird, he's been following us. . . . I finally went out and looked for him last night. I found him nestled in a bed of dandelions under a hawthorn bush. . . . He's a sort of changeling with bright blue eyes and berries in his hair. He has pointed ears and the rosiest cheeks you've ever seen. They look like little hearts pulsing under his skin. . . . I know, I know, I sound like a lunatic, but I've seen him. He smells like cinnamon and has this wonderful rippling laugh like a grown man . . .

TURNER *(Suddenly freezing)*: SSSSHHHHHHHH!

CHARLOTTE *(In a whisper)*: What is it?

TURNER: Nobody move.

CHARLOTTE: *Turner . . . ?!*

TURNER: Listen.

Dead silence.

CHARLOTTE *(In a whisper)*: I don't hear anything.
WALLY: Neither do I.
TURNER: Shhhhh! Quiet!

Pony starts to whimper in fear.

WALLY, CHARLOTTE AND TURNER *(Whispered)*:
Pony . . . !

She stops. Dead silence.

TURNER *(Barely audible)*: There it is again.
WALLY: *What?*
TURNER: The earth is turning.
WALLY: What are you talking about?
TURNER: Shhhh!

Silence.

PONY *(In a whisper)*: I hear it.
WALLY: It's something outside the tent.
PONY *(Barely audible)*: It's bears. Big. Black. Bears!
WALLY: An animal of some kind.
CHARLOTTE: Oh, I hear it too!
WALLY, TURNER AND PONY *(To Charlotte)*: SSHHH-
HHH!
TURNER: It's the humming of the spheres . . .
WALLY: Raccoons!
CHARLOTTE *(In a whisper)*: It's someone with a limp.

Pony whimpers.

TURNER: . . . suns and planets moving through space . . .
CHARLOTTE: They're coming closer!
PONY *(Clinging to Charlotte)*: It's the boogeyman, it's the
boogeyman!

WALLY *(Prepared for the worst)*: Stand back!
TURNER *(Transported)*: It sounds like people singing . . .

They freeze as we all hear a wondrous faraway sound. Charlotte gasps.

PONY: I hear it, I hear it!
CHARLOTTE *(Enchanted)*: Oh, Turner . . .
TURNER: What did I tell you?
WALLY: Only you . . .
CHARLOTTE *(Murmuring)*: Turner, Turner . . .

SCENE 3

The Blossoms have just reached a spectacular lookout high up in the Blue Ridge Mountains. It's a perfect afternoon one day and 122 miles later. Standing with them are Randy Wands with his three-week-old baby, William, strapped to his chest. They're all gazing at the view, frozen with awe. Nothing happens for several moments. Charlotte takes a deep breath. Wally focuses his camera. Turner beats his chest. Pony plucks a nearby wildflower. Silence.

CHARLOTTE: Oh Wally . . .

Turner yodels like an ape.

WALLY *(Snaps his picture)*: Got it!
RANDY *(Turning so William can see the view)*: Well William, what do you think?

Pony eats the flower.

WALLY: The Blue Ridge Mountains . . .
CHARLOTTE: Look . . . ! *(She sighs deeply)*
RANDY *(To William)*: Pretty impressive, eh what?
WALLY: . . . one of the oldest land areas on earth.

Turner beats his chest and yodels again. Pony joins him.

WALLY: We're talking over four hundred million years here. The Fertile Crescent was still underwater.

RANDY *(To the others)*: This is his first time up here.

CHARLOTTE: You can see forever.

RANDY: You think this is something, you ought to see it after a snowfall. It's like standing on top of the North Pole. White . . . white . . . white!

CHARLOTTE *(Hands over her ears)*: Kids, please?!

Turner and Pony stop.

RANDY: Forget the sledding . . . ! My wife and I have already bought him one of those aluminum numbers that looks like a satellite dish. Woooosh . . . ! I can't wait! My daddy used to bring me up here when *I* was little. We'd ease down on that old Flexible Flyer and go belly whopping all the way to Nashville and back. My mother'd have to pry us off with a crowbar . . . and then summers we'd come up here with chili dogs and soda and play our harmonicas. He was good, he was real good. When he got going, the bears would come popping out of those bushes and start stomping their feet like there was no tomorrow . . . !
(He pulls out a harmonica and plays a few lively measures)

PONY: My brother plays too.

RANDY: No kidding?

PONY: He's a prodigy. His name is Turner Blossom.

TURNER: *Pony . . . ?!*

WALLY: Now Pony . . .

RANDY *(Handing him the harmonica)*: Well, come on, let's hear you do your stuff!

TURNER: I play the guitar.

PONY *(More and more braggy)*: The classical guitar. He's been touched by God. *(She plucks another wildflower and starts eating the petals)*

TURNER *(Blazing with embarrassment)*: Pony?!

WALLY *(To Pony)*: Easy honey . . . and take that flower out of your mouth. What is this with suddenly eating flowers all the time?

PONY *(She quickly swallows it)*: He goes to Juilliard and everything.

TURNER *(To Pony)*: Will you stop it?

PONY: He's even played with symphony orchestras.

TURNER *(Lunging after her)*: I'm going to kill her!

WALLY *(Trying to restrain him)*: Easy, easy . . .

PONY: My daddy's a composer. His name is Wallace Blossom.

WALLY: All right Pony, cool it.

PONY: He teaches at Juilliard.

RANDY: Well, you sound like quite a family.

PONY: He wrote *The Atlantic Suite.*

A pause.

RANDY *(Trying to place it)*: *The Atlantic Suite* . . . ?

PONY *(Eager)*: Have you heard it?

WALLY: Pony, enough is enough!

PONY: It's played all over the world.

WALLY: Rio and Tokyo are hardly the whole world, and that was three years ago.

CHARLOTTE *(To Wally)*: Now, now . . .

RANDY: Well, William, it looks as if we've stumbled into some pretty fancy company here.

Charlotte sneaks a look at William.

WALLY: No, make it four . . . four and a half, to be more accurate. And at the rate I'm going, it'll be twenty years before I come up with something else. *(He goes and stands by himself)*

CHARLOTTE: Wally . . . ?

RANDY: So, where are you folks from?

CHARLOTTE: Hastings, New York. *(To Wally)* Honey . . . ?

RANDY: Say, you wouldn't know Panda Orenstein, would you?

CHARLOTTE: Panda Orenstein . . . ?

RANDY: Tall, red hair . . . she drives a green pickup truck . . . ?

CHARLOTTE: I know a Panda Vogel, but not a Panda Orenstein. Sorry.

RANDY: Great legs! I was real sweet on her once. Whoooie, that Panda Orenstein was something else! *(Pause)* So, where are you heading?

CHARLOTTE: Taos, New Mexico. *(She glances at William again)*

RANDY: *New Mexico?!*

CHARLOTTE: We're driving across the country to visit my aunt.

PONY: Olivia Childs, the famous artist who builds fabric mounds and circles in the desert.

TURNER *(Turning his back)*: I don't know her.

RANDY *(To Charlotte)*: Your aunt is Olivia Childs . . . ? *(To William)* Did you hear that William, these people are related to Olivia Childs.

PONY: She just finished a circle of one thousand kites.

RANDY: Right, right, I read about it in the paper. What's it called . . . ?

CHARLOTTE AND PONY: "Ring of Prayer."

RANDY: That's right, "Ring of Prayer" . . . a giant circle of snow-white kites.

WALLY *(Rejoining them with his camera)*: Come on guys, I want to take a picture of you up here.

RANDY: How does she come up with that stuff? Decorating the desert with sails and parachutes and wedding veils . . . ?

CHARLOTTE: Her pieces mark sacred Indian sites.

RANDY: But don't they blow away?

CHARLOTTE: That's the whole point—the risk of losing it all before the photographers get airborne. Her work celebrates its vulnerability to nature. . . . Prayer is eternal, but our shrines are made of air.

WALLY *(Waving at his family)*: Scrunch together!

CHARLOTTE *(Gazes at sleeping William and whispers)*: What a beautiful baby.

RANDY: Why thank you.

CHARLOTTE *(Touching his face)*: His *skin*...!

WALLY *(Motioning to Charlotte)*: Come on guys, let's have a little cooperation here.

CHARLOTTE *(To Randy)*: How old is he?

RANDY: Just three weeks.

WALLY: *Sweetheart...?*

CHARLOTTE: Can't you see I'm involved in something else?

WALLY: If we want photographs of this trip, someone's got to take them.

CHARLOTTE *(To Wally)*: All right, all right. Come on kids, Daddy wants to take a picture of us.

RANDY: Well, I hope you have a great time with that aunt of yours. She sounds like quite a woman.

PONY: She's dying of cancer.

CHARLOTTE: *Pony...?!*

RANDY: I'm so sorry, that's the worst...

CHARLOTTE *(Pulling the kids closer)*: Tell me about it.

WALLY *(Shaking his head)*: Please!

RANDY: ... the worst!

Charlotte heaves a deep sigh. Palace St. John, a hearty woman in her sixties, and Fletcher, her deaf grandson, join them and gaze out at the view.

CHARLOTTE *(Nodding towards Wally)*: He lost both his parents last year. Both!

PONY: She may not even be alive when we get there.

RANDY: To every thing there is a season, and a time to every purpose under heaven.

An uncomfortable silence.

RANDY *(Undaunted)*: A time to be born, and a time to die, a time to plant and a time to pluck up that which is planted...

WALLY: Okay guys, say "cheese."

They mournfully say "cheese."

WALLY: Come on, smile!

They try again, forced.

CHARLOTTE: Honestly dear, your sense of timing . . . !

Fletcher approaches Wally and reaches for his camera with authority.

PALACE: Let my grandson take it so you can be in it too. He's a whiz with cameras.
WALLY: Yeah? *(He hands it to him)* Well, thanks a lot.

Charlotte suddenly rips open her blouse and starts fanning herself.

CHARLOTTE: God, it's hot up here!
WALLY: Charlotte . . . ?
TURNER: Mom . . . ?!

Fletcher snaps away.

RANDY: Take it off, take it off!
WALLY: . . . what *are* you doing?
RANDY *(Laughing)*: I love it, I love it!
CHARLOTTE *(Fanning herself with both hands)*: Well, I guess these are the hot flashes my doctor was warning me about, though I still say I'm much too young to be going through this.
WALLY *(Indicating she's exposed)*: Honey . . . ?
CHARLOTTE *(Quickly buttons herself back up, laughing)*: Oh, sorry, sorry . . . *(To Fletcher)* Sorry.

Fletcher starts arranging them into a classic family portrait.

WALLY *(Hushed)*: She's right, the boy *is* good!
PONY: This is so fun!
WALLY *(To Charlotte)*: Now we'll really have something to show for this crazy escapade of ours.

Fletcher suddenly pulls Pony away from the others and places her in her own special row in front. He then snaps the picture and hands the camera back to Wally.

WALLY: Thanks a lot, that was terrific.

CHARLOTTE: Yes, you're really wonderful. Say thank you, kids.

TURNER: Thank you.

PONY: More, more!

CHARLOTTE: Now Pony.

PONY *(Pulling on Fletcher)*: More, more . . . !

PALACE *(Hugging him)*: Yes, Fletcher has quite an eye . . .

RANDY: Well, William, we better head back home or Mom and the twins will think we've run away to join the circus.

CHARLOTTE *(Gazing at William again)*: Kids, you've got to come see this baby, he's awake now.

PONY *(Joining her)*: Ohhh, he's so cute!

PALACE: He's just beautiful.

RANDY: Here, let's get you out of this thing so everyone can get a good look at you.

WALLY *(Chucking William under the chin)*: Well hi there, bright eyes, what's happening?

CHARLOTTE: He's precious.

RANDY: Say thank you, William.

CHARLOTTE: Just precious!

PONY: Look at his fingers, they're like candy corns.

WALLY *(Talking baby talk and making faces)*: Is someone trying to smile, hmmm? Yes, yes, yes . . . ! *(He makes more faces)*

RANDY: Well, William, is everyone admiring you?

WALLY: Yes! You can do it. Let's see those rosy gums . . .

RANDY *(Lowering his head into William)*: Willie, Willie, Willie! *(He makes loud buffling noises into the baby's stomach)*

WALLY: YES! LITTLE BABY. Ba ba ba ba ba! Little cheeks! What have you got in here . . . ? Tennis balls?

TURNER *(Pulling on Wally's sleeve)*: Easy, Dad, easy . . .

WALLY *(Recovering)*: Sorry, sorry . . .

CHARLOTTE: He really is spectacular.

PONY: Aren't you afraid he's going to break?

PALACE: Babies are very strong.
FLETCHER *(Signs to Palace)*: What day was he born?
PONY: *He's deaf . . . ?!*

The Blossoms and Randy stare open-mouthed at Fletcher.

CHARLOTTE AND WALLY *(Catching themselves, to Pony)*:
Shhhhh!
PONY *(In a whisper)*: Sorry, sorry . . .
CHARLOTTE *(Quietly)*: Honestly, Pony!

An awkward silence.

PALACE: He wants to know when his birthday was.
RANDY *(Too loud)*: JULY 7TH!
PALACE *(Signs back to Fletcher)*: July 7th.
CHARLOTTE: July 7th? That's Livvie's birthday! *(To Randy)*
Olivia Childs. She just turned eighty-one. Did you hear that
Wally? The baby was born on the same day as Livvie. What a
coincidence!
FLETCHER *(Signs to Palace)*: What time was he born?
PALACE: He wants to know what time he was born.
RANDY: Six thirteen AM. ELEVEN POUNDS, THREE
OUNCES.
PALACE *(To Randy)*: You don't have to yell, he can't hear you
anyway.
RANDY *(Mortified)*: Right, right . . . *(To Fletcher)* Sorry about
that.
PALACE *(Signs to Fletcher)*: Six thirteen AM. Eleven pounds,
three ounces.
PONY: Ohhh, I want him, I want him!
WALLY: He's a great baby.

A silence as they all gaze at William.

FLETCHER *(Touches William's head and signs)*: He will be a
leader of men.

PALACE: He says William will be a leader of men.

FLETCHER *(Signs)*: Your son was born under a highly elegant and aristocratic confluence of the planets.

Palace translates. Everyone gapes at Fletcher.

FLETCHER *(Signs)*: Because he was born on the seventh day of the seventh month, he's a totally evolved Cancerian who'll operate in large social dimensions.

Palace translates.

RANDY: Oh William, listen . . . !

FLETCHER *(Signs)*: His whole being cries out for the common good.

Palace translates.

FLETCHER *(Signs)*: He'll not only lead, he'll also create— forging bold new philosophies of tolerance and trust.

Palace translates.

RANDY: You hear that, William?

FLETCHER *(His signing gets more and more expansive)*: Like a precious jewel flung into a pond, his imprint will shiver and reverberate long after he's gone.

Palace translates.

FLETCHER *(Signs with foreboding)*: But be warned . . .

Palace translates.

CHARLOTTE: Oh no . . .

RANDY: What, what?

FLETCHER *(Signs)*: He will have to pay a price for these gifts . . .

Palace translates.

WALLY: I knew it!
CHARLOTTE *(Hands over her ears)*: I can't listen.
RANDY: What, what? Tell me!
FLETCHER *(Signs)*: His natal moon is in Scorpio, the demon sign . . .

Palace translates.

FLETCHER *(Signs)*: Just as he moves to better mankind, the scorpion's poison will flood his senses . . .

Palace translates.

RANDY: Stop, stop!
FLETCHER *(Signs)*: He'll be racked with jealousy and desire . . .

Palace translates.

RANDY: Please!
FLETCHER *(Signs)*: But all is not lost . . .

Palace translates.

FLETCHER *(Signs)*: Because of your son's fortunate trine aspect, he will vanquish the powers of darkness and walk in eternal light.

Palace translates. Silence.

RANDY: Did you hear that, William? You're going to be a great man. I knew it, I knew it! *(He covers him with kisses)*
CHARLOTTE: Ohh, that was amazing, just amazing!
TURNER: How does he know all that?
PALACE: Fletcher's a psychic. He can read destinies through any medium . . . astrology, cards, palms . . .

PONY *(Pulling on Charlotte's arm)*: Oh, have another baby, Mommy. Have another baby!

RANDY: It's the way he expressed it.

PALACE: Yes, Fletcher's quite a boy. *(She signs to him)* They're all very impressed with you.

PONY: It would be so fun.

TURNER: Yeah, have another.

RANDY *(Puts William back in his carrier)*: Well, William, we'd better make tracks or Mom will be calling the ranger station.

PONY *(Pulling on Charlotte)*: Please?

TURNER: Please?

RANDY *(Shakes Palace's hand)*: It was a pleasure meeting you folks, and as for your grandson here, he's real special, real special! *(He squeezes Fletcher's arm, then waves to the Blossoms)* Be good. *(And he's gone)*

PONY: We'd help you take care of it.

CHARLOTTE: What's all this about having babies all of a sudden?

TURNER: Come on . . .

PONY: Ohhh, maybe it would be twins!

TURNER: Or triplets!

WALLY: Hey, hey, give your poor mother a break here.

PONY: Oh triplets! Go for it Mommy!

CHARLOTTE *(Laughing)*: Please!

PALACE: I had five myself. *(She signs to Fletcher)* Her kids want her to have more babies.

FLETCHER *(Signs)*: Babies are great.

PALACE *(Speaking and signing at the same time)*: Babies *are* great, but they're a lot of work. *(To the others)* There are long stretches of time I have absolutely no memory of.

PONY: It would be so neat. Babies in the kitchen, babies in the hall, babies rolling down the stairs . . . *(Clinging to Charlotte)* Goo goo, gaa gaa . . . goo goo, gaa gaa *(Etc.)*

TURNER *(Likewise)*: Babies in the yard, babies pouring out of the faucets . . . waa waa, waa waa *(Etc.)*

WALLY: Come on kids, cool it.

CHARLOTTE: I'm afraid it's too late.

PALACE: It's never too late. My mother had me when she was forty-seven. She didn't even know she was pregnant. She thought she had the flu.

PONY: Please? Pretty please?

CHARLOTTE: I can't.

PALACE: Who says you can't?

WALLY: Her body says she can't.

Charlotte breaks away from them.

PALACE: Oh, I'm so sorry.

Signing, she leads Fletcher away.

PALACE: Come on, sweetheart, I'll explain later.

PONY: What's wrong with Mommy?

Charlotte weeps and weeps.

TURNER: Mom, are you okay?

CHARLOTTE: Oh Wally, I can't bear it . . . I'll never feel life moving inside me again . . .

WALLY *(Arms around the kids)*: Hey, hey, you've still got Turner and Pony . . .

CHARLOTTE *(Racked)*: No, no, you don't understand . . .

WALLY *(Not moving)*: Honey, honey . . .

CHARLOTTE: It's like . . . like part of me's dying. . . . The best part.

SCENE 4

Wally and Turner are fly-fishing side by side in a mountain stream in Asheville, North Carolina. It's late afternoon the next day. Wally's wearing beat-up old hip boots and his fishing hat. Turner's barefoot in shorts and a light jacket. A liquid calm prevails.

WALLY: This is heaven . . . heaven!

TURNER: You said it.

WALLY: No one here except you and me. *(Pause)* And of course the fish.

TURNER: Fish are great.

WALLY: Fish *are* great! *(He casts)* Boom!

TURNER: They're so weird! What are they, anyway?

WALLY: Souls. Departed human souls.

TURNER: Come on . . .

WALLY: We begin life in water, so it's where we end up.

TURNER: Where did you get that? *(He casts with too much force)*

WALLY: Common sense. Our souls have to go somewhere. Oceans and streams are the only places left with any room, so they turn into fish. No, no, just flick your wrist like this. *(He demonstrates)* See? Flick!

Turner does a sloppy repeat.

WALLY: Don't *throw* it out. Just toss it out. It's all in the wrist. *(He demonstrates again)* Flick . . . flick . . . flick!

TURNER: Wait a minute, are you saying that all those trout darting around down there were once people?

WALLY: You got it. *(He casts again)* See that?

TURNER: That we'll be cooking up some bank robber or dead housewife for dinner?

WALLY: I hardly moved my arm at all. Bank robber, Indian brave, Joan of Arc . . . it could be anyone.

TURNER: And that I'm going to end up as a guppy or goldfish? That I'll spend all eternity swimming around in some kid's grimy fishtank . . . ?

WALLY: Not necessarily . . . you could get lucky and end up as a swordfish or twelve-ton tuna swimming off the coast of Bali. And it's not forever. You keep changing species . . . stingray one year, smallmouth bass the next . . .

TURNER *(Casts so violently he accidentally throws his pole into the water)*: Whoops!

30

TINA HOWE

WALLY: JESUS, TURNER!
TURNER *(Scrambles to pick it up)*: Sorry, sorry . . .
WALLY: I SAID: DON'T THROW IT!
TURNER: I'm sorry.
WALLY *(Reaching it first)*: That's a two-hundred-dollar rod and
   reel you've got there!
TURNER: I'm really sorry.
WALLY *(Wipes if off)*: Son of a bitch! *(A silence as he inspects it)*
   Well, you were lucky this time.
TURNER: It just flew out of my hands.
WALLY *(Handing it back to him)*: Okay, here you go.
TURNER *(Doesn't take it)*: No, I think I'll just watch.
WALLY: Come on, take it.
TURNER: I like watching you.
WALLY *(Forcing it on him)*: Will you take it?!
TURNER: Okay, okay . . .
WALLY: I've finally got a chance to teach you something I'm
   really good at, so take advantage of it!
TURNER: Okay.

Silence.

WALLY: I happen to be an ace when it comes to fly-fishing.
TURNER: I know.

Silence.

WALLY: So pay attention.
TURNER: Okay, I'm with you.
WALLY *(Picking up his rod again)*: It's like making music. The
   whole thing is to stay loose. *(He casts)* See that?
TURNER: Nice!
WALLY: Boom!
TURNER: Very nice, Dad.
WALLY: Just put it right out there!
TURNER *(Prepares to cast)*: All right fish: say your prayers.
WALLY: And . . .

TURNER *(Casts much better)*: Boom!

WALLY: Yes!

TURNER: I did it!

WALLY: It's all about the fine art of letting go.

TURNER *(Reeling in the line)*: This is fun.

WALLY: It's like when I was writing *The Atlantic Suite*. I could do no wrong. The melodies just kept coming. Adagios and obbligatos unfurled all around me. Cadenzas shivered overhead, fanfares swelled underfoot. . . . I wrote them down as fast as I could. It was amazing. Incredible! *(He casts again)* Boom!

TURNER: Or my spring recital at Juilliard. I was in a trance. It was so weird, I had the feeling my fingers had turned into a flock of parakeets or canaries. . . . I kept expecting to see all these feathers floating out over the audience. *(He makes eerie sound effects then casts beautifully)*

WALLY: Then poof, it was all over. Granddad and Mamie both got sick, I was put in charge, and ashes, ashes, we all fall down. Though I can't blame everything on them. I just lost it, that's all. It can happen to anyone. The trick is to accept it and go down gracefully, right old buddy? Blub, blub, blub . . . *(Casts too vehemently and gets the line tangled)* Whoops!

TURNER: Hey, I think I got it!

WALLY *(Struggling to untangle it)*: Shit!

TURNER: Watch, Dad!

WALLY: Goddamnit!

TURNER *(Casts perfectly)*: Boom!

WALLY *(Making a worse and worse mess of it)*: What's wrong with this fucking line?

TURNER: Did you see that?

WALLY: I knew that guy sold me the wrong weight!

TURNER: Dad . . . ?

WALLY: Stupid asshole!

TURNER: I can do it now.

WALLY: You can do *what*?

TURNER: Cast.

WALLY: Well, any idiot can cast if they have the right line!

TURNER: Want to see?

WALLY *(Doubled up over his reel)*: Do you believe this?!

TURNER *(Casts perfectly)*: And . . . boom!

WALLY *(Tearing the line off the reel)*: We drive thirty miles to go fishing in this great secluded mountain stream and what happens . . . ? The goddamned line breaks on me! . . . *Unbelievable!*

TURNER *(Offering him his rod)*: Here, use mine.

WALLY: I don't want yours.

TURNER: Come on, take it . . .

WALLY: I said: *I don't want it!*

TURNER: But you were doing great.

WALLY: No, *you* were the one that was doing great, not me.

TURNER *(Trying to press it on him)*: Come on, Dad . . .

WALLY *(Pulls his line every which way, then finally flings his rod into the water)*: Oh fuck it! Just fuck the whole goddamned thing!

TURNER *(Offering his rod again, eyes filling with tears)*: Dad . . . ?!

SCENE 5

Midnight, two days and seventy miles later. The Blossoms' tent is nestled in a moonlit clearing high up in the Smoky Mountains. Everyone's asleep except for Charlotte, who's sitting stock still, straining to hear something. It's pitch black and eerie woodland sounds abound. A baby suddenly cries.

CHARLOTTE *(In a whisper)*: Wally . . . ? *Wally?*

WALLY *(Half asleep)*: Uuuhhhh . . .

CHARLOTTE: Listen!

WALLY: Uuuhhhh . . .

CHARLOTTE: There it is again.

The crying stops and then resumes, sounding less and less like a baby.

CHARLOTTE *(Getting out of her sleeping bag)*: It's the baby.

WALLY *(Waking up)*: Hey, where are you going?

CHARLOTTE: He's been crying all night.

WALLY *(Grabbing her arm, amorous)*: I was just dreaming about you.

CHARLOTTE: I'll be right back.

WALLY: Hey, hey, not so fast! *(He tries to pull her into his sleeping bag)*

CHARLOTTE *(Resists, laughing)*: Honey . . . ?!

WALLY: Come here.

CHARLOTTE: What are you doing?

WALLY: Trying to get you into my sleeping bag.

The crying becomes more and more catlike.

CHARLOTTE: Wait! . . . Listen!

WALLY: Sweetheart, it's a stray cat! *(Nuzzling against her)* Mmmm, you smell so good!

CHARLOTTE *(Resisting)*: Wally . . . ?!

WALLY *(Pulling her into his bag)*: Come on, get in here. I never get to be alone with you anymore.

Thuds and crashes as he tries to haul her in.

CHARLOTTE: Honey, there isn't room . . . ! Gosh, you're right, that does sound like a cat!

WALLY: Mmmm, you're so warm! *(A crash)* Whoops!

CHARLOTTE: Shhh! You'll wake the kids.

WALLY *(Trying to pull off her top)*: Come on, let's get this off. *(He accidentally pokes her in the eye)*

CHARLOTTE: Ow!

WALLY: Sorry, sorry . . .

CHARLOTTE: You hit me in the eye.

WALLY: I'm sorry. There. Is that better?

CHARLOTTE *(She starts to giggle)*: I don't believe this!

WALLY: Here, lift up a little.

Pony moans in her sleep.

CHARLOTTE *(Sitting up like a bolt)*: What was that?

WALLY *(Trying to get at her legs)*: What have you got on here?

CHARLOTTE: Shhh!

WALLY: Hiking boots?

CHARLOTTE *(In a whisper)*: Turner, is that you?

WALLY: Since when did you start wearing hiking boots to bed? *(He drops one to the ground)*

Pony moans again.

CHARLOTTE: Turner . . . ?

WALLY: Goddamned sweatpants! *(He gets them off)* Ahhh, this is more like it!

CHARLOTTE: Take off your shirt.

WALLY: Talk to me, talk to me.

They embrace, laughing and groaning. Pony moans again.

CHARLOTTE: Honey, we're waking up the kids.

WALLY: Fuck the kids!

CHARLOTTE: WALLY?!

WALLY: What do you think families did in the old days when everybody slept in one room?

CHARLOTTE: This isn't the old days.

WALLY: Our Founding Fathers didn't have separate bedrooms and look how well they turned out! Mmmm, you're so soft! I'd forgotten how soft you were!

CHARLOTTE *(Trying to break away)*: I just can't in front of them . . .

Wally croons with pleasure.

PONY *(Whimpering in her sleep)*: Stop, stop! I didn't do it, I didn't do it!

Charlotte struggles to get out of the bag.

WALLY: Hey, where are you going?

PONY: No, no . . . put it down. . . . Melinda's in the kitchen
with the ocean player.

CHARLOTTE: Turner's having a nightmare.

WALLY: Kids have nightmares. And that isn't Turner, it's Pony.
(Getting out of his sleeping bag, pulling her with him) Come on,
let's get out of here!

CHARLOTTE: Wallace . . . ?!

WALLY: Let's take a walk.

CHARLOTTE: But what about the kids?

PONY: Eeewwwww, there's a spider, look out, look out!

WALLY: They're asleep.

CHARLOTTE: And what if they wake up?

WALLY: They won't.

CHARLOTTE: How do you know?

WALLY: Because they never wake up in the middle of the night.

CHARLOTTE: Wally, you've lost your mind!

WALLY *(Grabbing her arm)*: Come on, let's go.

CHARLOTTE: Honey, you don't leave two small children alone
in the middle of the Smoky Mountains!

WALLY: Don't we have any rights around here?

CHARLOTTE: I don't believe this!

WALLY *(Getting madder and madder)*: I mean, isn't this our
vacation too?

CHARLOTTE: Shhh shhh, not so loud!

WALLY: What about us for a change? You and me?

CHARLOTTE: Oh God . . . !

WALLY: You only care about them!

CHARLOTTE: That isn't true.

WALLY: It is so! It's always the kids this, the kids that . . .

CHARLOTTE *(Trying to hush him)*: Honey, please . . . ?!

WALLY: See what I mean? *(Heading for the door)* Look, you can
stay chained to them if you want, but I'm taking a walk!

CHARLOTTE *(Following him to the door)*: Wally . . . ?

WALLY: I don't even care if you come with me or not. *(And he's
gone)*

CHARLOTTE: Honey, please! Now what do I do . . . ? *(She
lurches back and forth between the door and the sleeping kids)* Oh

shit! *(Then grabs a blanket and flashlight and rushes to the door)* Wally, wait up . . . ! *(Running back to the kids)* Please God, don't wake up. . . . Just . . . *don't! (And she's gone)*

A long silence, then spooky sounds start up. Wings flap, the baby cries and cries, an albino bat gives birth to kittens. Pony moans in her sleep. A lion roars close by.

PONY *(Wakes like a shot)*: What was that?

Silence. Then all the sounds combine into a terrifying cacophony.

PONY *(In a whisper)*: Mommy?

The sounds get louder.

PONY: *Mommy . . . ?!*

And louder.

PONY *(Frozen)*: It's bears!

Dead silence.

PONY: MOOOOOOOOOOOOOOMYYYYYY???!
TURNER *(Wakes instantly)*: What's happening?
PONY: It's bears. Big black bears!

Silence.

TURNER: I don't hear anything.

The lion roars again.

TURNER *(Whispering)*: Dad . . . ?
PONY *(Whispering)*: Mommy . . . ?
TURNER: Is that you?

PONY: Can I get in with you?

TURNER: It's so dark in here.

PONY *(Creeping out of her sleeping bag)*: Where are you?

TURNER *(Likewise)*: Who has the flashlight?

PONY: Mommy . . . ?

TURNER *(Running into Pony)*: Dad . . . ?

PONY: No, it's me, Pony.

TURNER: *Pony . . . ?*

PONY: What?

TURNER: Oh no!

PONY: *Turner . . . ?*

TURNER: Where are they?

Silence.

TURNER: DAD . . . ?	PONY: MOMMY? . . .
DADDY . . . ?	MOMMMYYYYYYY?

Silence.

PONY: *The bears got them, the bears got them!*

TURNER: Will you shut up?

PONY: I want Mommy, I want Mommy!

TURNER: Come on, quiet down or they'll get us too!

An instant silence.

PONY *(Jumping)*: What was that?

TURNER: What was what?

PONY: *That!?*

TURNER: I didn't hear anything.

PONY: It sounded like snakes.

TURNER: Will you stop it?

PONY: It's snakes, it's snakes!

TURNER: Wait a minute, let me get my circus light.

He turns on the kind of little fiberoptic flashlights sold at circuses and starts waving it, drawing liquid circles in the air.

PONY: Oh neat! Let me try.

TURNER: Use your own.

PONY: I don't know where it is.

TURNER: Look in your sleeping bag. *(He keeps waving it)*

PONY: Hey, I found it, I found it! *(She turns it on and copies Turner)* This is fun.

TURNER: I wish we had sparklers.

PONY: Oh, sparklers would be great!

They wave away until the tent starts to glow.

PONY: Hey, why don't you play your guitar.

TURNER: Now?

PONY: It would be neat.

TURNER: Yeah?

PONY: Yeah, we'll have a sound-and-light show. I'll do them both and you play that really beautiful piece . . .

TURNER *(With enthusiasm)*: Okaaay! *(He hands her his light and starts taking his guitar out of its case)*

PONY: Are you scared of seeing Livvie?

TURNER: Why should I be scared?

PONY: Because she's dying of cancer.

TURNER: So?

PONY: She'll look all strange. Her teeth will be black and she'll be wearing a wig.

TURNER: How do you know?

PONY: I heard Mommy and Daddy talking.

Turner starts playing Bach's Suite No. 1 in G Major. Pony listens for several measures, then resumes waving the lights as Turner plays.

PONY: What if she dies in front of us? What if she turns blue and starts gasping for air . . . ? *(She makes lurid strangling sounds)* What if she wants to be alone with one of us? What if we're locked in the room with her and she comes after us . . . ? What if she falls and dies right on top of us . . . ?

There's a sudden awful noise outside.

PONY (*Dropping the lights*): IT'S HER, IT'S HER.... SHE'S COMING TO GET US!

Turner continues playing.

PONY: HELP . . . HELP . . . !
TURNER (*Stops playing*): Jeez, Pony!
PONY: She's coming to get us, she's coming to get us!
TURNER: She lives over two thousand miles away!
PONY: Mommy, Mommy . . . !
TURNER (*Rising*): I'm getting out of here, you're crazy!
PONY: Hey, where are you going?
TURNER (*Heading for the door*): I want to see what's going on.
PONY: You can't go out there.
TURNER: Who says?
PONY: The bears will get you! (*In a frantic whisper*) Turner . . . ?!
TURNER (*Pulls back the tent flap and steps outside*): Ohhh, look at all those stars!

Moonlight pours through the door.

PONY: Turner, get back in here!
TURNER: The sky's full of shooting stars. Quick, Pone, you've got to see this!
PONY (*Whimpering*): I want Mommy, I want Mommy . . .
TURNER (*Returning for Pony*): They're amazing. Come on, give me your hand.
PONY: Where are we going?
TURNER: Just follow me.

He leads her to a clearing outside the tent. The sky is ablaze with shooting stars.

TURNER (*Putting his arm around her shoulder*): Well, what do you think?
PONY: Ohhhhh, look!

TURNER: Isn't it incredible?

PONY: Look at all those stars!

TURNER *(Pointing)*: Oh, one's falling, one's falling!

PONY: There are millions of them . . .

TURNER: Did you see that?

PONY: . . . billions and zillions of them!

TURNER: Come on, let's get closer.

PONY: Ohhh, they're so bright!

Arms around each other, they walk deeper into the starlit night.

TURNER: Hold on tight now. I don't want to lose you.

The curtain slowly falls.

Act Two

SCENE 1

It's four days and 700 miles later. The Blossoms are in a sailboat scudding across a lake in Oklahoma City with Charlotte's brother, Scotty Childs; Joy, his new wife, who's African-American and seven months pregnant; and Amy, his daughter from his first marriage. Amy's at the tiller wearing a Little League shirt and cap. She looks suspiciously like a boy. The grownups are drinking champagne and laughing. Pony's sitting close to Joy waiting to feel the baby move, and Turner's sunbathing on the deck. The wind slaps against the sails as they skim over the water. It's one of those idyllic summer days you remember for a lifetime.

SCOTTY *(Laughing)*: Wait, wait, there's more . . .
JOY: You and Charlotte packed a fourteen-inch cast-iron frying pan . . . ?
SCOTTY: . . . a fourteen-inch cast-iron frying pan, an orange-juice squeezer, an electric toaster . . .
JOY: But Scotty, how did it all fit in a doll's trunk?
ALL *(Roaring with laughter)*: It didn't!
CHARLOTTE: *Plus* . . .
WALLY: Plus a gallon of milk, a bottle of maple syrup . . .
TURNER: Three jars of peanut butter . . .
PONY: Four-and-a-half bananas . . .
AMY: Five bags of marshmallows . . .
CHARLOTTE: And Horatio, my life-size pink teddy bear!

JOY *(Laughing)*: Stop, stop . . . !

WALLY *(Hopping up with his camera)*: Nobody move! I've got to get a picture of this! *(He starts snapping away)*

SCOTTY: And of course . . . the crucial carton of eggs.

CHARLOTTE: Yes, don't forget the eggs.

TURNER, PONY AND AMY: The eggs, the eggs, the eggs!

WALLY *(Snapping away)*: OH YES!

CHARLOTTE: Which all smashed when I tried to shut the lid.

AMY: *Yuck!*

PONY: Eeewy gooey, eeewy gooey.

JOY: This is the saddest story I've ever heard.

SCOTTY: What do you mean?

CHARLOTTE: It's not sad.

JOY: Running away from home to fry eggs on top of a mountain . . . ?

SCOTTY: We were city kids. *(Tilting the champagne bottle)* A little refill, Char?

CHARLOTTE: We wanted to join Livvie out West. She'd built herself this canvas dome high up in the Tetons. It was the shape and color of a giant apricot. It was that crazy dome that inspired Scotty to move out here and become a landscape architect. *(Holding out her glass)* Please!

SCOTTY *(Pouring)*: It's true. I still remember the pictures of it. It was a cross between a hot-air balloon and a mad scientist's observatory . . .

WALLY *(Taking more pictures)*: What a day . . . ! It's days like this that make you feel you can do anything.

CHARLOTTE: She wanted to be close to the sky . . .

WALLY: Swim the Atlantic, ride bareback on a zebra, write music that will leave audiences sobbing in their seats. It's all just . . . *out there,* swaying within reach.

CHARLOTTE: This was in her painting days before she moved to the desert . . . which she says is even closer to the sky.

WALLY: The thing is to seize it! *(He roars with resolve)*

JOY: I understand wanting to run away to join her . . .

WALLY: Thrust out your arms and partake!

JOY: But to fry eggs . . . ?

SCOTTY: She made great eggs. *(Lifting the bottle towards Wally)* Wallace?

CHARLOTTE: She made *great* eggs!

WALLY: Please! *(Extending his glass)*

Scotty fills it.

JOY: When I ran away from home, it was to CBS in Chicago because I wanted to be a newscaster so badly.

CHARLOTTE: You were just more realistic, that's all. *(Mopping her brow)* Gosh, it's hot out here!

JOY: The only problem was, it was over five hundred miles away, and it took me four days to get there.

WALLY *(Drinks in great gulps)*: Crawl out of your hole and partake!

CHARLOTTE: But look how it paid off! I mean, here you are interviewing kings and presidents all over the place.

JOY *(Jumps, hand over her stomach)*: WHOA!

PONY: I felt it, I felt it! *(She presses her head against Joy's stomach)* Again, again!

CHARLOTTE: Our dream was to make it out West and fry eggs with wild-and-woolly Livvie . . . *(She fans herself)*

SCOTTY: We would have walked across Siberia to be with her.

WALLY *(Flings his head back and closes his eyes)*: Ahhhh!

CHARLOTTE *(With affection)*: Look at Wally . . . ! *(Taking his hand)* Having fun, sweetheart?

WALLY: This is the life.

Charlotte leans against him and sighs happily.

WALLY: Everything is music. All you have to do is listen.

PONY *(Pressing her head into Joy's stomach)*: Neato! I can hear it breathing. *(She breathes loudly)*

JOY: *Her,* not it! She's a girl. Your mommy wove her the most amazing quilt covered with dragonflies . . .

PONY: It's a girl? How do you know it's a girl?

JOY: Because I had a special test. Really Charlotte, you could show your things in art galleries . . .

WALLY: That's what I keep saying.

JOY: They're so beautiful.

CHARLOTTE: Please! It's just a hobby.

PONY: What kind of a test?

JOY: A test where they take out some of the fluid the baby is living in.

PONY: Ewwwww, ewwwwwww!

JOY: It doesn't hurt.

CHARLOTTE *(Quietly to Scotty, shifting away from Wally)*: So, when did you see Livvie last?

SCOTTY: Amy and I flew up two weeks ago. She's becoming quite a little pilot.

CHARLOTTE: You go all the way to Taos in the Cessna?

SCOTTY: It's a snap. With favorable winds we can make it in three hours.

JOY: Babies live in special sacs filled with water.

CHARLOTTE: And how was she?

SCOTTY: Not good.

WALLY *(To Charlotte)*: Come back, come back.

PONY: Then how do they breathe?

JOY: Through gills. They start out like fish.

AMY: Ewwwww . . . ewwwww!

CHARLOTTE: Yeah, she sounded pretty rocky on the phone the other day.

SCOTTY *(Voice lowered)*: It's just a matter of days.

CHARLOTTE *(Hands over her ears)*: Don't . . .

SCOTTY: You'll make it in time, don't worry.

CHARLOTTE: Oh Scotty . . . !

SCOTTY: I know, I know. *(He takes her hand)*

CHARLOTTE: Well, racing to finish "The Ring of Prayer" in a-hundred-and-two-degree heat didn't help. Sybil was furious with her.

SCOTTY: What would we do without that woman? She's not only a great doctor, but she and Sinclair are the only ones Livvie will listen to.

CHARLOTTE: I don't know which I dread more—getting there too late or having to see her suffer.

SCOTTY: The worst is over, it's just a matter of letting go.

CHARLOTTE: Stop . . .

JOY *(To Pony)*: You see, nature is very logical. Since life began in water, we begin in water too. When a baby's tiny it looks just like a fish. Then it grows hair and lungs and turns into an egg-bearing mammal . . .

PONY: Wow . . . !   AMY: Gee . . . !

PONY: You mean, *I* was a fish?

JOY: We all were! *(She makes fish faces and laughs)*

PONY *(Yelling over)*: HEY TURNER, DID YOU KNOW WE ALL STARTED OUT AS FISH?

TURNER: No, we *end up* as fish, silly.

A silence.

SCOTTY: Hey, Amy, how about giving someone else a turn?

AMY: Sure, anyone want to sail?

PONY *(Raising her hand)*: Oh me, me!

SCOTTY: Turner?

TURNER: I don't know how.

AMY: Come on, I'll teach you. It's easy.

SCOTTY: She's an ace, she's been sailing since she was two. Go on, give it a whirl.

Turner joins her.

PONY *(Softly to Charlotte)*: Amy is so weird. Are you sure she's not a boy?

CHARLOTTE: Now Pony . . .

AMY *(Showing Turner)*: This is the tiller. It's like a steering wheel, except you move it in the opposite direction you want to go. *(She moves it from side to side)* See? It's a cinch.

JOY: The girl's amazing. She's captain of the track team, she plays first base for Little League, and don't ask me where this came from—but she's a crackerjack at archery!

CHARLOTTE: Well look at her mother . . .

SCOTTY: You look at her!

WALLY: What's old Inge up to these days?

AMY *(Handing over the tiller)*: Now you try.

SCOTTY: Running marathons, if you can believe it.

PONY: Mommy . . . ?

WALLY: You're kidding.

SCOTTY: She's gone off to Calcutta to train.

WALLY: Calcutta?

JOY: No, no, Kenya. He mixes them up on purpose.

SCOTTY: So, to continue our saga . . .

PONY: Mommy . . . ?

JOY: Yes, do, do!

CHARLOTTE: It just gets worse, believe me.

WALLY: Hey, Turn, how're you doing?

TURNER: Great!

AMY: He's a natural!

PONY: *Mommy?!*

WALLY AND CHARLOTTE *(Angry)*: What is it, Pony?

PONY: This is fun.

SCOTTY: Good girl! That's just what I like to hear . . . *(He tousles her hair)* So, after Char smashed the eggs trying to close the doll's trunk, we realized we had too much stuff. We decided not to bring anything.

PONY *(Snuggling up to Joy again)*: You're so pretty.

JOY: Why thank you, honey.

PONY: I love your hair. *(She starts playing with it)*

JOY: Ugh, you can have it! *(To the others)* What I can't get over is that your parents let you go.

CHARLOTTE: They were very liberal.

JOY: If I lived in New York City and Amy suddenly announced she was going to run away from home to fry eggs on top of the Tetons, I wouldn't let her out the door!

SCOTTY: Well, there were two of us, remember.

JOY: But you were only eight and eleven . . .

PONY *(Still involved with Joy's hair)*: Can I brush it?

JOY: . . . you were just babies! *(Starts rummaging around in her bag)* Sure, I think I've got a brush in here someplace . . .

TURNER: LOOK EVERYBODY, I'M SAILING, I'M SAIL-
ING!

CHARLOTTE *(Waving to him)*: Yay Turner . . . !

AMY: Tomorrow I'm going to teach him how to windsurf. That's
really fun!

WALLY *(Getting out his camera and taking more pictures)*: Wait'll
they see this back at Juilliard . . . Turner at the helm. And
suddenly he's surrounded by a herd of killer whales.

AMY *(Pointing into the distance)*: Thar she blows!

JOY *(Finds a brush and gives it to Pony)*: Here you go.

PONY *(Brushing away)*: Ohhh, it's so curly! I wish I had hair like
this!

JOY *(With disgust)*: Please!

AMY *(Grabbing Turner)*: Look out, look out, one's right under-
neath us! Man the lifeboats! *(She starts running up and down)*

AMY AND TURNER: MAN THE LIFEBOATS! MAN THE
LIFEBOATS!

SCOTTY: Easy Amy, easy. *(Pause)* So . . . we announced our
plans on a bright Sunday morning in April. Father said it was
fine with him, and he gave us a couple of dimes in case we
wanted to call from the road. Mother just warned us not to talk
to strangers . . .

JOY *(To Scotty)*: Incredible!

CHARLOTTE *(Fanning herself)*: And never to accept anything
from them.

JOY *(Noticing Charlotte's discomfort)*: Hey, are you okay?

CHARLOTTE: Particularly soda. *(To Joy)* It's this brutal Oklahoma sun.

SCOTTY: She said wicked people sometimes pour poison in it
when you're not looking so they can rob you. She then told us
to be back by 1:30 for lunch because . . . *(A weighty pause)*

SCOTTY AND CHARLOTTE: "We're having chocolate
sundaes for dessert!"

CHARLOTTE: Oh Scotty, I wish you didn't live so far away!

SCOTTY *(Reaching for it)*: Hey, how about another bottle of
champagne?

WALLY *(Putting his camera away)*: Sounds good to me! *(He suddenly starts humming the woodwind section of a melody that's come to him)*

SCOTTY *(Uncorking the bottle as he talks)*: We headed into Central Park, figuring that was the best place to start looking for mountains.

CHARLOTTE: I would have followed him anywhere, *anywhere!*

JOY *(To Pony)*: Would you like me to brush *your* hair? It's so pretty. It shines like corn silk.

PONY: Sure!

JOY: My little sister and I used to do this for hours. . . . Hours! *(She brushes Pony's hair into a series of fancy styles)*

SCOTTY: And before we knew it, we were standing in front of the lion's cage at the zoo. *(Lifting the bottle in Charlotte's direction)* Char?

CHARLOTTE: Please!

SCOTTY *(Fills her glass, then moves towards Wally)*: Maestro?

WALLY: Let 'er rip! *(He keeps humming his melody)*

Charlotte starts sprinkling herself with drops of champagne.

SCOTTY *(Pouring)*: That's my man! If you come up with some new quartet or symphony on this boat, *I* expect some of the credit now . . .

WALLY: You got it. *(Tilts his glass to him and drinks)* Ahhhhh . . .

JOY *(To Pony)*: How about we sweep it all on top of your head and make you look like a princess?

PONY: Ohhh, that feels so good. Isn't Joy beautiful, Mommy?

CHARLOTTE *(Guiltily stops dousing herself)*: Very.

JOY: Please! I'm a blimp!

CHARLOTTE: In fact, Joy's one of the most beautiful women I know.

SCOTTY: Hear, hear. . . . So, there we were watching the lion pace back and forth when this man suddenly comes up to us and says, "You children aren't out here all alone, are you?"

JOY: Oh God . . . !

CHARLOTTE: Naturally we don't answer him since Mother told us not to talk to strangers . . . *(She pours more champagne into her glass)*

SCOTTY: But then he looks really concerned and asks, "Have you lost your mother and father . . . ?"

JOY *(Skeptical)*: Right, right . . .

CHARLOTTE: No, he seems genuinely concerned, so we say, "No, we're running away from home."

JOY: Oh no!

SCOTTY: So *he* says, "You're running away from home, are you? Where are you going?"

JOY: I can't listen to this!

CHARLOTTE: So, *we* say, "To the top of a mountain to fry eggs with Livvie!" *(To Scotty)* We really *were* crazy, you know. *(She dunks her hand in her glass and sprinkles more champagne over herself)*

SCOTTY: And *he* says, "Gosh, that sounds like fun. Can I come with you?"

JOY: Stop . . .

CHARLOTTE: So we say, "Sure." *(Pause)* This is really great champagne.

JOY: These things really scare me.

WALLY *(Draining his glass)*: This *is* great champagne!

SCOTTY *(Handing him the bottle)*: Help yourself, I've got lots more on board . . .

WALLY *(Refills his glass)*: Ahhh, just what the doctor ordered. . . . You were absolutely right Char, this has turned out to be a terrific trip, really terrific! *(He lets out a roar and tilts the bottle Charlotte's way)* How about some more?

CHARLOTTE: Thanks. . . . So, there we are telling this guy about all our plans while the lion keeps pacing back and forth in his cage . . . *(She douses her arms and shoulders directly from the bottle)*

SCOTTY: We're going on and on about how we're going to hook up with our crazy Aunt Livvie who paints twelve-foot canvases of clouds and sky, when he suddenly says, "You know, we're standing in a very vulnerable spot in relation to this lion because of the wall behind us. If he suddenly decides to take a leak, it's going to hit the wall and ricochet all over us like a loose fire hose."

JOY: Scotty, this is getting weird.

SCOTTY: The guy then launches into this lecture about the great force with which lions pee, and how the wall behind us will just act as a conductor. So Char and I start to get a little nervous. I mean, this is *not* the sort of conversation we're used to . . .

Charlotte is now pouring the champagne all over herself.

SCOTTY: When all of a sudden, the lion looks us straight in the eye, lifts his leg, and lets fly the most horrendous piss you've ever seen! We are talking broken water main here. . . . It comes streaking past us at ninety miles an hour, slams into the wall just as the guy predicted and—SPPPPLATTTTTT!—we are drenched! I mean, soaked from head to foot!

JOY *(Laughing)*: Oh no.

CHARLOTTE *(Pouring the champagne over her head)*: It was unbelievable!

WALLY: *Honey . . . ?!*

SCOTTY: Charlotte, what are you doing?

A silence as they all stare at her.

CHARLOTTE *(Guiltily hides the bottle behind her)*: Oh, sorry, sorry . . . I was a little hot.

WALLY: Then you go in for a swim. You don't waste good champagne.

SCOTTY: Hey, how often do I get to see my little sister?

CHARLOTTE *(Mopping herself off)*: Sorry, this is a new thing with me. It's like I'm on fire all the time.

WALLY: Jesus.

JOY: That's some story . . . !

SCOTTY: It's not over yet.

JOY: Oh no.

SCOTTY: We made it back to the apartment just as Mother was filling our milk glasses.

JOY *(Laughing)*: I don't believe a word of this.

CHARLOTTE: Father took one look at us and said, "Good Lord, what happened to you on top of that mountain? It looks as if a lion peed all over you!"

She and Scotty roar with laughter.

JOY: He followed you.

CHARLOTTE *(Still laughing)*: He followed us.

WALLY: It's such a wonderful story.

SCOTTY: Father worked in mysterious ways.

CHARLOTTE: You can say that again. *(Pause)* We had a great childhood.

SCOTTY: A great childhood!

CHARLOTTE: The best.

WALLY *(To Turner)*: HEY SKIPPER, HOW'S THE WHALE SITUATION?

TURNER: We scared them all away.

WALLY: That's my boy! Just look at him. The kid can do anything, anything! *(He roars with pride)*

TURNER: Let's us get a boat!

CHARLOTTE: Oh, Turner, Turner. . . . Why do I love little boys named Turner so much?

JOY *(Has finished Pony's hairdo)*: There, you're done. You're one beautiful little girl, you know that? *(She gives her a big kiss)*

PONY *(Prancing up and down)*: Look at me, look at me!

SCENE 2

Early evening, two days and 230 miles later. Turner and Pony come running out of the Panhandle Diner thirty miles east of Amarillo, Texas. They head for the car, Pony pretending she's Wally, and Turner pretending he's Charlotte.

PONY *(Sliding behind the wheel)*: COME ON GUYS, GET A WIGGLE ON!

TURNER *(Gets in next to her)*: It would be nice to reach a campsite before dark for once!

PONY *(Yelling out her window)*: KIDS . . . ? *(To Turner)* What's your cash situation like?

TURNER *(Yelling out his window)*: LET'S GET MOVING! *(To Pony)* Eighty-five cents.

PONY: Great, that's just great! I have a dollar fifty! *(Pretends to turn on the ignition)* Well, let's just hope we've got enough gas to make it to Armadillo.

TURNER: Amarillo, *Amarillo!*

PONY: Jesus, Char, what are those kids up to? We paid the check ten minutes ago. *(Yelling out the window)* PONY . . . ?!

TURNER: TURNER . . . ?!

PONY *(Softly)*: What do you say we take off without them?

TURNER: Now you're talking! Come on, step on the gas!

PONY *(Making accelerating sounds)*: Those kids are history!

Charlotte and Wally come streaming out of the diner—Charlotte pretending she's Turner and Wally pretending he's Pony.

WALLY: Mommy, Mommy, Mommy . . . ?!

CHARLOTTE *(Getting into the car behind Turner)*: They're leaving without us!

WALLY *(Clambering in next to her)*: Mommy, Mommy, Mommy . . . !

PONY: Shit!

TURNER: They caught up with us.

PONY: Just our luck!

TURNER *(Turning around, all smiles)*: Hi kids.

PONY: Son of a bitch!

WALLY: No fair, Turner's in my seat!

CHARLOTTE: I am not!

WALLY: You are so!

CHARLOTTE: Am not!

WALLY *(Starts pounding on Charlotte)*: Give me my seat back!

CHARLOTTE *(Hitting back)*: Cut it out, Pony!

WALLY: OW, OW, TURNER'S HITTING ME, TURNER'S HITTING ME!

TURNER: Careful of his hands now. . . . Come on Wally, *do* something! I can't take this anymore.

Charlotte and Wally keep slugging each other.

PONY: *You* can't take it . . . ? What about me? I'm having a fucking nervous breakdown!

WALLY: You're so mean, you're so mean . . . OW . . . OW. . . . No fair!	CHARLOTTE: I'm going to kill you, Pony, I really mean it!

It escalates.

TURNER: KIDS, KIDS. . . . ENOUGH IS ENOUGH!	PONY: IF YOU DON'T STOP IT RIGHT THIS MINUTE, I'M GETTING OUT OF THE CAR!

PONY: THAT'S IT . . . ! WE'RE TURNING AROUND AND GOING BACK HOME!

TURNER: Sweetheart?

PONY: This vacation is over!

WALLY: I'm sorry, we'll be good, we'll be good.

PONY: It's too late.

TURNER: But what about Livvie?

WALLY: Daddy's mad. I hate it when Daddy's mad.

PONY: Livvie, Livvie . . . everything's always Livvie. You're on the goddamned phone with her every other day!

CHARLOTTE: Don't worry, he'll get over it.

TURNER: I had another one of my dreams last night. I finally found the baby I keep hearing crying outside the tent.

PONY: Oh no, not another one of your crazy dreams!

TURNER: I picked him up and brought him inside to show you.

WALLY: I've got to pee.

CHARLOTTE: So do I!

TURNER: And he was enormous! So big I could hardly carry him.

WALLY: *Mommy?!*

TURNER: Except it wasn't a baby and it wasn't a boy.

CHARLOTTE: We've got to pee!

PONY: Easy kids, easy . . .

TURNER: It was Livvie. She'd been buried alive . . .

WALLY AND CHARLOTTE: We've got to pee, we've got to pee, we've got to pee!

PONY: Buried alive . . . ? *(Whirling around)* I said: CAN IT!

They do.

PONY: Thank you. *(To Turner)* And . . . ?

TURNER: She was all covered with mud and leaves and stuff and she was roaring with laughter, saying "Hubba-hubba, hubba-hubba." Shaking and sputtering, with tears rolling down her face, saying it over and over again. "Hubba-hubba, hubba-hubba, hubba-hubba!" *(Pause)* It was terrifying.

WALLY: I miss Spit and Wheat Germ!

WALLY AND CHARLOTTE *(In a loud wail)*: Spitty, Spitty, Spitty, Spit!

PONY *(Under her breath)*: This is a fucking madhouse!

TURNER *(Softly)*: Wally, I *wish* you wouldn't use that kind of language in front of them!

PONY: I mean, after a while . . .

WALLY: Mommy . . . ?

TURNER *(Fanning himself)*: Jeez, it's hot in here!

PONY: . . . how much can a guy take?

CHARLOTTE: Dad, can I move up front with you?

WALLY: Mommy?

PONY *(To Charlotte)*: No, you can't move up front with me!

TURNER *(Taking off his shirt)*: I don't know about the rest of you, but I'm burning up!

CHARLOTTE: Please?

PONY: I said, no!

Turner starts fanning his naked chest.

WALLY: Mommy . . . ?
PONY *(To Turner)*: Charlotte, what *are* you doing?
TURNER: I'm hot!
WALLY: *Mommy . . . ?!*
TURNER AND PONY: WHAT IS IT, PONY?
WALLY: This is fun! *(He grabs a candy bar out of Charlotte's pocket)* Nyah, nyah, I've got your candy bar. Anyone want some?
CHARLOTTE *(Trying to snatch it back)*: Hey, that's mine!

They start fighting.

CHARLOTTE: Ow, ow, watch my hands . . . ! *(She lifts them up and examines them)* Jeez, Pony!
PONY *(Suddenly gets out of the car, slamming the door behind her)*: I CAN'T TAKE THIS ANYMORE, YOU DRIVE!
TURNER: Honey . . . ?
CHARLOTTE *(Starting to get out)*: Great! Now I can sit up front!
WALLY *(Pulling her back)*: Oh no you don't! It's *my* turn to sit up front! *(Starts slugging her)* TURNERRRR?!

They fall into another fight.

PONY *(Storms to the back of the car and gets in behind the driver's seat, pushing Wally over and Charlotte out)*: MOVE!
CHARLOTTE *(Falling with a crash)*: OW!
WALLY: Daddy, what are you doing?
CHARLOTTE *(Dashes over to Turner's door and starts pushing him towards the driver's seat)*: Move over, Mom! *(Back to Wally)* Nyah nyah, I got here first!
TURNER *(Being pushed behind the wheel)*: Turner . . . ?!

WALLY *(Storms out the backseat after Charlotte)*: Oh no you don't . . . ! *(And gets into the front seat, shoving Charlotte behind the wheel and Turner out onto the ground)*

TURNER: Hey . . . ? What's going on?

CHARLOTTE: Jeez, Pony!

WALLY: No fair, no fair!

PONY: This is more like it, now I have the whole backseat to myself!

TURNER *(Comes around to the back and pushes Pony over)*: That's what you think! Move over!

Turner slams his door, Wally slams his, Pony slams hers and Charlotte slams her.

CHARLOTTE *(To Wally)*: Hi Pone.

WALLY *(To Charlotte)*: Hi Turn.

PONY: GREAT IDEA! LET THE KIDS DRIVE!

TURNER *(Stunned)*: What?

CHARLOTTE *(Turning on the ignition)*: Far out!

WALLY: Go for it, Turner!

TURNER *(To Pony)*: They can't drive!

PONY: Who says?

TURNER: Honey, you've lost your mind.

PONY: I don't know why we didn't think of this before. It solves everything!

CHARLOTTE *(Gunning the gas pedal)*: And . . . we're off!

SCENE 3

Taos, New Mexico, two days later, around noon. The Blossoms have just been ushered into Olivia Childs' bedroom by Dalia Paz, her Mexican nurse. Pony clings to Charlotte's skirt, terrified. Turner's next to her, carrying his guitar. Olivia's fourposter bed dominates the room. It's shrouded with masses of fabric, making it look like a gauze cathedral about to lift off the ground. A vase of orchids sits on her bedside table and an oxygen hookup is nearby.

DALIA: Come . . . she is expecting you. *(She sweeps across the room and lifts the gauze around the bed; to Olivia)* Ya llegaron, Señora. [They are here, Señora.]

Olivia doesn't stir.

DALIA: She sleeps and sleeps. *(Waving them closer)* Please . . .

Wally and Charlotte gingerly step forward.

PONY *(Being pulled with them)*: No, no, no, no . . .
CHARLOTTE *(Taking Olivia's hand)*: Livvie . . . ? Livvie? It's me, Charlotte.

Pony keeps whimpering.

DALIA: Your family is here, Señora. Wake up, wake up. They want to see you.
CHARLOTTE *(Softly)*: How are you feeling?
DALIA *(To Olivia)*: Vamos, abre los ojos. Han venido de muy lejos. [Come, open your eyes. They have traveled a long way.]
CHARLOTTE: That's all right, let her sleep.
DALIA: No, no she sleeps too much. Despiertate, despiertate! Estas muy caprichosa! [Wake up, wake up! You're being very naughty!]
CHARLOTTE: We can come back later.
DALIA *(Angry to Olivia)*: Asi es como te vas a comportar cuando tu familia te viene a visitar? [Is this how you behave when your family comes to see you?]

Nothing.

PONY: She's dead, she's dead!

CHARLOTTE: PONY . . . ?!	WALLY: Can it, Pony, just can it!	TURNER: God, Pony!

CHARLOTTE *(To Dalia)*: She's too young to understand.
DALIA *(Not understanding)*: Please?
CHARLOTTE: I said . . . she doesn't understand.

Dalia looks at her blankly.

CHARLOTTE *(Embarrassed)*: She thinks she's dead.
DALIA *(Upset)*: Oh no, no, Señora! She is not dead! Don't say
such things. She is sleeping.
CHARLOTTE: I know, I know . . .
DALIA *(Mimes sleeping for Pony)*: She is sleeping.
CHARLOTTE *(Voice lowered)*: She's too young to understand,
she's just a baby.
DALIA: Yes, she sleeps like a baby. She's my little angel. *(She
strokes Olivia's forehead and murmurs)* Y en dónde estas ahora,
mi querida? Nadando en una playa azul como un pescadito, o
volando más alto que las nubes como una grande aguila? [And
where are you now, my precious one? Swimming in the clear
blue ocean like a little fish? Or flying high above the clouds like
a great eagle?]

Silence as the Blossoms stare at the floor.

DALIA *(Noticing Turner's guitar)*: You play the guitar?
TURNER: Yes.
DALIA: I play too.
TURNER: Yeah?
DALIA *(All modesty)*: Just a little.
TURNER: That's great.
DALIA: Not great just . . . so-so . . .
TURNER: Come on, I'll bet you're really good.
DALIA *(Blushing)*: No, no . . .
WALLY: Play for us!
TURNER: Yes, do! *(He hands her his guitar)* Come on . . .
CHARLOTTE: We'd love to hear you.
DALIA *(Stroking it)*: What a beautiful guitar.

CHARLOTTE: And it might help wake her up.

DALIA: It's been so long, so long . . . I used to play and dance in the hills . . .

She bends over it, takes a deep breath and starts playing and singing a spectacular flamenco song complete with hand slapping and Gypsy yelps. The Blossoms stare at her, open-mouthed, then gradually thaw, snapping their fingers and tapping their feet. Wally suddenly starts to dance. Charlotte joins him in a torchy duet. Then the kids join in, feigning a bullfight. They get more and more carried away.

DALIA *(Finishes in an inspired burst and hands the guitar to Pony)*: Gracias.

The Blossoms break into wild applause.

TURNER *(Staring at Dalia)*: That was amazing!

WALLY: Spectacular!

Olivia moans.

DALIA: She's awake! *(She goes over to her)* Señora, ellos llegaron. [Señora, they are here.]

OLIVIA *(Groggy)*: Music . . . I heard music.

DALIA *(Propping Olivia up)*: Anda, anda. . . . Abre tus ojos. [Up, up. . . . Open your eyes.]

Olivia is raised to a sitting position. She's terribly old and frail, to the point of transparency. She opens her misty eyes. The Blossoms gasp.

PONY *(In a whisper)*: She's alive!

Olivia abruptly shuts her eyes and sinks back into her pillows.

TURNER *(To Pony)*: Now look at what you did.

PONY *(Terrified)*: I'm sorry, I'm sorry . . .
CHARLOTTE: Oh Wally, I didn't think she'd be this bad.
DALIA *(Pulling her back up)*: Señora, no sea caprichosa. Quieren verte. Han venido de muy lejos. [Señora, don't be naughty, they want to see you. They've come a long way.] Open your eyes!

Olivia opens her eyes and looks around blankly.

DALIA: See? They're here!
OLIVIA *(To Dalia)*: Who are these people?
CHARLOTTE *(Leaning over her)*: It's me, *Charlotte!*
DALIA: Your family, my angel!
CHARLOTTE *(Taking her hand)*: Oh Livvie, it's so good to see you again. You look wonderful.
OLIVIA *(Peering at Charlotte)*: Scotty?
CHARLOTTE: No, it's me, *Charlotte*. Scotty's in Oklahoma City.
WALLY: You look great!
CHARLOTTE: Doesn't she?
OLIVIA *(Suddenly spies Turner)*: Amy!
CHARLOTTE: No, no, this is Turner.
OLIVIA *(Stretching out a bony arm)*: Amy, Amy, come closer and let me get a good look at you.

Pony whimpers in terror.

CHARLOTTE: Livvie, it's me, *Charlotte*. This is my son, *Turner!*
OLIVIA *(Gesturing more frantically)*: Closer, I can't see you!
PONY *(Clutching on to Wally)*: Daddy, Daddy . . . !
CHARLOTTE *(Shepherding them closer)*: Come on kids, you're too far away . . .
WALLY *(Pulling her forward)*: Pony . . . ?!
PONY *(Digging in her heels)*: No, no, no . . .
CHARLOTTE *(To Olivia)*: See, it's me, Charlotte, and here are my two children, Turner and Pony . . .
OLIVIA *(Snatches Turner's hand)*: Amy . . . ! Come, give your poor old great-aunt a kiss like a good little girl. *(She makes lurid kissing noises)*

Turner freezes and Pony whimpers.

OLIVIA: Don't be frightened, I won't bite.

Turner leans over and gives her a quick peck on the cheek. Pony's whimpering gets louder.

WALLY *(Under his breath)*: Stop it, Pony! Just . . . stop it!

OLIVIA *(Gazing at Turner)*: I can't get over how much she looks like a boy.

CHARLOTTE *(Getting the giggles)*: Oh God . . .

OLIVIA: Why do you cut her hair so short and dress her this way?

DALIA: Señora, this *is* a boy!

WALLY *(Under his breath, referring to Dalia)*: Obviously she hasn't met Amy!

He and the kids start to giggle.

CHARLOTTE *(Chastisingly)*: Wally!

OLIVIA *(Pulling Turner closer)*: You're such a pretty little girl. Why don't you let your hair grow?

CHARLOTTE: Livvie, this is my son, *Turner*! He's going to play for you later.

OLIVIA: Ah yes, you play baseball, don't you?

The Blossoms' giggles increase.

TURNER: Come on, guys . . .

PONY *(Swinging Turner's guitar)*: Batter up. . . . Play ball!

OLIVIA *(Notices Pony for the first time)*: And who is this?

TURNER: My sister.

OLIVIA *(Seeing her with the guitar)*: So you were the one playing the music just now . . .

DALIA: That was me.

TURNER: No, I'm the one that plays.

OLIVIA: I didn't know you had a sister that played the guitar. Well, well . . .

DALIA: No Señora, *I* was playing . . . *(To the others)* She gets confused sometimes.

OLIVIA *(To Pony)*: You play very well.

PONY: Thank you.

Olivia suddenly falls back into her pillows, eyes closed, mouth open. Silence.

CHARLOTTE: Maybe we ought to let her rest awhile, I'm afraid we're tiring her out.

WALLY: Good idea.

CHARLOTTE *(Starts moving towards the door, voice lowered)*: Come on kids, we'll come back later.

DALIA *(Fussing over Olivia)*: Duerme, mi ángel. Volveran. [Sleep my angel. They'll be back.]

WALLY *(Herding the kids towards the door)*: Quietly, quietly . . .

PONY: Shhhhhhhhh . . .

CHARLOTTE *(Whispering to Dalia)*: We'll see her after lunch.

DALIA *(Crooning to Olivia)*: Descansa, mi querida. Vuelve a tus sueños. [Rest, my sweet one. Go back to your dreams.]

The Blossoms start tiptoeing out the door. Olivia suddenly sits up, thrusting out an arm.

OLIVIA *(In an agonizing cry)*: NO, NO, DON'T GO! DON'T LEAVE ME!

SCENE 4

Later that evening, around nine. A bedside lamp glows eerily in Olivia's room. She's being examined by her doctor, Sybil Wren, a hearty woman in her sixties who has a severe limp. Wally, Charlotte and Dalia stand nervously in the doorway. Turner and Pony are spread out in the hall playing Hearts.

SYBIL *(Stethoscope on Olivia's chest)*: All right now, take a deep breath.

She takes a shallow one.

SYBIL: Hold it.

She does.

SYBIL: Okay, you can let it out.

She does.

SYBIL: Again.

They go through it again.

SYBIL: Good, Now cough.

She coughs weakly.

SYBIL: Again.

And weaker still.

SYBIL: And once more.

It's barely audible.

SYBIL: Oh Liv, what are we going to do with this poor tired-out old body of yours?
OLIVIA *(In another world)*: No, no, just back up the truck over by the canyon . . .
SYBIL: How's the pain?
OLIVIA *(Agitated)*: Why would I bring candles? The shovel's under the porch. OW, OW . . . STOP IT! THAT HURTS!
SYBIL: I know, I know . . .
OLIVIA: STOP IT, YOU'RE CRUSHING MY CHEST! *(She whimpers)*

Sybil kisses Olivia's brow, puts away her stethoscope, snaps her bag shut.

SYBIL *(To the others)*: I almost thought she'd lick it.

CHARLOTTE *(Leaning against Wally, weepy)*: I can't bear it, I just can't . . .

WALLY: Oh honey . . .

SYBIL: She's such a crafty old bird.

Dalia lurches out of the room with her hands over her face.

CHARLOTTE *(Suddenly breaks away, weeping)*: Oh Wally, it all goes so fast . . .

SYBIL: She's always got one more trick up her sleeve.

WALLY: Honey . . . ?

CHARLOTTE: I'm sorry, I'm sorry, I just can't keep up . . .

SYBIL *(To Olivia)*: Come on, show us your stuff.

CHARLOTTE: You dance through childhood, race through the teenage years, fall in love a couple of million times, bear some delicious bald babies, and then . . . whhhhhhst, it's all over. . . . Don't you ever feel like digging in your heels and shouting, "SLOW DOWN GUYS AND LET ME GET THE LAY OF THE LAND FOR A MINUTE!" . . . *(She pauses and looks around the room)* It's nine o'clock in the evening . . . the children are playing cards in the hall . . . there's a sweet smell in the air. What is it? Pistachios! The whole room smells of pistachios . . . ! Livvie's sleeping with her mouth open. Look at her. Poor thing, she looks like an old man. . . . Just slow down and take it all in. . . . Sybil's wearing silver earrings, Wally's got a bruise on his arm, someone's heart is beating like crazy. . . . Shhh! Listen! . . . Lub dub, lub dub, lub dub, lub dub. . . . It's *my* heart! Nobody move. . . . The moment's holding. . . . *(In a whisper)* It's perfect . . . perfect . . . !

A silence.

OLIVIA *(Babbling)*: The children are in the meadow flying kites. . . . There's Franklin in his pinafore. Wait for me . . . wait for me . . . !

SYBIL: It's funny, I've been feeling real anger lately . . .

CHARLOTTE: Oh, Wally . . . !

SYBIL: I keep thinking about that first project I went on with Liv when I lost my leg. You know, her eight-mile highway of sails that wound around Chaco Canyon. The reason I lost it was because she was so intent that they all fly at precisely the same height. And that was no small task when you consider she used over three thousand sails rigged on forty-foot masts. . . . It was beautiful as hell, but backbreaking work. We were a crew of one hundred and fifty . . .

OLIVIA *(Overlapping)*: Come on Franklin, it's my turn. . . . Oh no, Boxer's loose, Boxer's loose! Bad dog, go back to Mummy!

SYBIL: I was rehoisting the last one five-and-a-half inches higher, and she just serenely backs the truck over me . . . I mean, here I take off time from medical school to help her on the project, and she runs over my leg for five-and-a-half lousy inches. Do you believe it?

OLIVIA: Wait, wait, I've got a stone in my shoe . . .

SYBIL: Well, the woman has me bewitched, I'd follow her anywhere. It's just lately I've been feeling this deep resentment. I mean, it's hard enough being a female doctor out here, but then to be a one-legged one on top of it . . .

CHARLOTTE AND WALLY: Sybil . . . !

Turner and Pony suddenly appear at the door.

CHARLOTTE: Oh, hi, kids!

A pause.

SYBIL: I'm not complaining, I'm not complaining. I have a wonderful life. Sinclair's a great husband and we have two fabulous children. . . . It's just there's so much more I wanted to do.

Turner and Pony edge over towards Wally.

WALLY: Yeah, I know what you mean. Our feelings play strange tricks on us. *(Putting an arm around each)* Oh, hi guys. This has been a tough year. The last thing I wanted to do was drive to New Mexico to watch another relative die. But the closer we got, the better I began to feel. I mean, look at us . . . we drove over two thousand miles and we're still talking to each other. We had a few laughs and saw some dynamite scenery. It was a great trip, a great trip! And here's poor Livvie hanging on by a thread, and I'm still raring to go. Charlotte's in another world, the kids are terrified, and you're furious . . .

PONY *(Gazing up at him)*: Hi Daddy.

WALLY: Hi Pone, what's happening?

OLIVIA *(Moaning in her sleep)*: Amy, Amy, I want to see Amy . . .

CHARLOTTE: What's she saying?

OLIVIA *(Garbled)*: The little girl who played the music . . .

WALLY: I think she wants to see Turner again.

OLIVIA *(Beckoning towards the kids)*: Closer . . . come closer!

WALLY: Go on Turner, she's calling you.

Turner starts to approach her.

OLIVIA: No, the other one. Bring me the other one.

CHARLOTTE *(Nodding in Pony's direction)*: Her?

WALLY: Pony?

TURNER: My sister?

OLIVIA *(Pointing directly at her)*: THAT ONE! The little girl with the glasses!

They all stare at Pony, who goes rigid.

WALLY: Well, Pone, I guess you're the one she wants this time.

PONY *(Frozen, barely audible)*: No, no, no, no . . .

SYBIL: Don't be afraid, she won't hurt you. *(Pushing Pony towards her)*

WALLY: Come on, Pone, there's nothing to be afraid of.

CHARLOTTE: Honey, she just wants to look at you.

PONY (*In a frantic whisper*): Turner, you promised you wouldn't leave me alone with her . . . *Turner* . . . ?!

WALLY: Atta girl . . .

CHARLOTTE: Honey, you're embarrassing us!

SYBIL: I was the same way at her age, exactly the same . . .

Olivia starts to chuckle in a terrifying way.

PONY (*Eyes closed*): She'll die on me, she'll die on me . . .

CHARLOTTE (*Horrified*): PONY . . . ?

PONY: HELLLLLLLLLLP!

Turner looks on helplessly.

OLIVIA (*Sounding more and more like a witch*): Yes, *she's* the one I want . . .

PONY (*Flinging her arms around him*): SAVE ME, TURNER . . . SAVE ME!

Wally and Charlotte pry her away.

TURNER: I'm sorry Pone, I'm sorry . . .

SYBIL: Don't be scared, she's gentle as a lamb . . .

Charlotte drags Pony, head bowed and eyes closed, to Olivia's bedside. A long silence as Olivia glares at her. No one breathes. Olivia suddenly stages a little show. She bleats like a lamb, howls like a coyote and crows like a rooster. She then rips off her wig, revealing a bald pate. Everyone screams. Dalia comes running into the room. Dead silence.

OLIVIA: I just wanted to make sure you were paying attention.

SYBIL: Typical, typical.

DALIA (*Crossing herself*): Santa María de la Cruz!

CHARLOTTE: Livvie!

WALLY: Whoa! You nearly gave me a heart attack!

Olivia then pulls off her bald pate, revealing a crop of sparse white hair which she coyly fluffs into place.

TURNER *(Starts applauding her)*: Wow! Way to go!

PONY: That was really neat!

OLIVIA: There, this is more like it.

SYBIL: See what I have to deal with? You can't trust her for a minute.

OLIVIA: Now there's a little life around here!

PONY: Again, again!

SYBIL *(To Olivia)*: And here we were practically administering last rites. You are very naughty!

OLIVIA: Well, a dying old lady's got to have some fun.

PONY: More, more!

CHARLOTTE: You're too much, too much!

PONY: Gee, you're really neat!

OLIVIA *(Sighs deeply and shuts her eyes)*: All right, now everybody leave the room.

DALIA *(Protesting)*: Señora . . . ?!

OLIVIA *(Pointing a stern finger)*: I said, go!

DALIA: But someone has to stay with you.

OLIVIA: You heard me. I want to be alone.

SYBIL *(In a whisper, moving towards the door)*: Come on, we'll wait outside the door.

OLIVIA *(Highly agitated)*: GO, GO, GO!

SYBIL *(Shepherding them all out)*: All right, all right.

They all tiptoe towards the door.

OLIVIA *(Pointing at Pony)*: Except for her! I want the little girl to stay.

PONY *(Amazed)*: Me . . . ? You want *me*?

OLIVIA: Yes. You stay!

PONY *(Happy)*: All right!

Everyone stares at Pony.

PONY: You heard her, we want to be alone.
SYBIL *(Starting to move)*: Okay okay, but if you need us, we'll be right outside.
DALIA: What about changing your bedclothes?
OLIVIA: *I said GO!* And shut the door behind you.
PONY: Yes, shut the door behind you.

Everyone leaves. Dalia shuts the door. A silence.

OLIVIA *(Closes her eyes, then opens them and smiles)*: There, this is more like it. Sit down, sit down.

Pony pulls up a chair next to her and sits.

OLIVIA *(Casually plucks an orchid out of her vase and starts eating it)*: Mmmmm . . .

Pony watches, amazed.

OLIVIA: Would you like to try one?
PONY: Could I?
OLIVIA *(Handing it to her)*: Please!
PONY *(Takes a cautious bite)*: Mmmm, I've never had this kind before. *(She eats with rising gusto)*
OLIVIA: They're orchids.
PONY *(Finishing it off)*: It's so sweet!
OLIVIA: An old admirer sends them to me from Hawaii. Here, have some more.

She hands Pony a few and takes more herself. They munch away, smiling at each other and wiping their mouths.

PONY *(Between swallows)*: How old are you?
OLIVIA: Eighty-one.
PONY: *Eighty-one . . . ?* Gosh, that's so old!

OLIVIA: And how old are you?

PONY: Nine.

OLIVIA: *Nine . . . ?* Is that all? I thought you were thirteen or fourteen . . .

PONY: No, just nine.

OLIVIA: I'm amazed!

PONY: When's your birthday?

OLIVIA: July 7th.

PONY: Oh, that's right. We just met a baby that was born on the same day. He was so cute. *(Pause)* What's your favorite color?

OLIVIA: White. And yours?

PONY: Blue.

OLIVIA: Blue's all right.

PONY: And what's your favorite animal?

OLIVIA: The snowy owl. And yours?

PONY: *Horses!*

OLIVIA: Horses. Of course!

PONY: Do you have a lucky number?

OLIVIA: One.

PONY: *One?* That's so weird.

OLIVIA: What's yours?

PONY: Four.

OLIVIA: How come?

PONY: I don't know, it just is.

Silence.

OLIVIA: I like your glasses. Could I try them on?

PONY: Sure. *(She takes them off and hands them to her)*

OLIVIA *(Putting them on)*: Ohhhh, these are great! Everything's so clear!

A silence as she gazes around the room.

PONY: How do you go to the bathroom if you have to stay in bed all day?

OLIVIA: In a bedpan.

PONY: What's that?

OLIVIA: A kind of portable toilet. Would you like to see it?

PONY *(Thrilled): Could I?!*

OLIVIA: Sure. *(She whips it out from under the covers and holds it aloft)* What do you think?

PONY: Oh, that's neat!

OLIVIA *(Handing it to her)*: Here, sit on it, it's like a little throne.

PONY *(Puts it on the seat of her chair and sits on it)*: Wow . . . ! *(She makes a peeing sound)* Pssssssss . . .

OLIVIA *(Offers her the first wig she had on)*: Now put this on for the full effect . . .

PONY *(Puts it on and tucks her hair inside)*: Pssssssss psssssss . . .

OLIVIA *(Starts laughing and clapping her hands)*: Perfect, perfect! *(She suddenly has a seizure and grabs for the oxygen mask)* Air . . . air . . . *(She gropes wildly to get it on)* Help me, I can't get it on, I can't get it on . . .

PONY *(Rises and gropes for the unit)*: Wait, I can't see . . .

OLIVIA: Air . . . air!

She finally gets it on. Her breathing becomes more labored. She takes several more deep breaths and is restored. She removes the mask and hangs it up. She gazes at Pony and smiles. A silence.

PONY: What happened?

Olivia shuts her eyes and sighs.

PONY: Are you okay?

OLIVIA *(Drifting off to another world)*: Come, let's move into the shade. I don't like all these bees.

PONY: I thought you were dying.

OLIVIA *(Waving her hands at the invisible bees)*: Shooo shoo . . .

PONY: Death is so scary. Aren't you scared? I don't want to die.

Olivia keeps shooing away the bees.

PONY: I get so scared thinking about it, I can't sleep. Every night I touch my bedside light forty-four times and hold my breath for as long as I can and pray, *"Please God, don't let me die! I'll be good, I'll be good!"* And then I start imagining what it will be like. . . . You know, being dead in a coffin, being underground all alone in the dark . . .

OLIVIA: What's that smell? I know, it's cloves. . . . Cloves!

PONY: . . . with mice and, and spiders, and worms crawling over me . . . and, and dead people moaning all around me . . . and trying to call Mommy and Daddy but they can't hear me because I'm so far underground . . .

Olivia breathes heavily.

PONY *(Getting more and more upset)*: And, and then I start thinking about being there forever and ever and ever and ever until my body's a skeleton . . . a clattery skeleton with grinning teeth and no eyes, and I touch my night-light 144 times so it will go away, and then 244 times, and 444 times, and I get crying so hard Mommy has to come in and hold me. . . . And, and. . . . Oh no, it's starting to happen now. . . . Could I get in bed with you? *(Climbs in next to her, whimpering)* I don't want to die, I don't want to die . . .

OLIVIA *(Waking, groggy)*: I just had the most beautiful dream . . .

PONY *(Clinging to her)*: Hold me, hold me!

OLIVIA: No, it was a reverie because it actually happened. Yes . . . it happened a long long time ago.

PONY: Tighter!

OLIVIA: I was on a train . . . *(She reaches for a nasal cannula that feeds her more oxygen)* Wait, just let me put this on, it helps me remember. *(Still in Pony's glasses, she puts it on)*

PONY *(Reaching out for her)*: Hold me!

OLIVIA *(Breathing easily)*: Ahhh, that's better, much better . . . I was on a train . . .

PONY *(Burying her head against Olivia, wig still on)*: I don't want to die, I don't want to die!

OLIVIA *(Putting her arms around her)*: There, there, no one's going to die. . . . I was on this horrid train on my way to the Sahara Desert. . . . Yes, there was something about the Sahara Desert back then. . . . I wanted to get lost in it, fling myself facedown in it. . . . I'd been studying painting in Paris for the year. How could I have forgotten . . . ? I was all of twenty. Mercy, this was a thousand years ago. During my wild days. *(She roars)* What I put my poor parents through! Well, you'll do it too, you'll do it all, just wait and see. . . . Poor thing, you're shivering . . .

PONY *(Whimpering)*: I don't want to die, save me, save me!

OLIVIA: What's all this talk about dying all of a sudden? . . . I was on a train somewhere between Paris and Tangier . . . we'd stopped at some godforsaken town in the middle of nowhere, and standing on the platform was the most beautiful man I'd ever seen—tall, with olive skin and a thrilling mouth. He wore a white suit and was pacing up and down the platform carrying this enormous bouquet of poppies that stained his face crimson. I couldn't take my eyes off him. He was like something out of *The Arabian Nights.* I kept expecting to see peacocks and jeweled elephants stamping in the distance. Finally he caught my gaze . . . I pressed my face against the window and whispered, "My name is Callisto!" *(She laughs)* Do you believe it? I used to call myself Callisto in those days. . . . The train suddenly started up. We pulled out of the station. I watched him get smaller and smaller. Then I fell into a deep sleep. I began having nightmares . . . I was being chased down this long tunnel . . . I started to scream. Someone grabbed my hands. I opened my eyes. It was him! He'd jumped on the train at the last minute and was sitting across from me, eyes laughing, poppies blazing. . . . He didn't speak a word of any language I knew, but he held me spellbound. I never made it off the train. He wrapped me in his flying carpet and wouldn't let me go. You've never seen such feverish carryings-on. . . . He rocked me over mountains, sang me through rain forests and kissed me past aancient cities. Oh, what a ruckus we made! Well, you'll do it too, you'll do it all, wait and see. We ended up in Zanzibar, island of cloves. *(She removes her nasal cannula)* I was so full of him, I thought my heart would

burst. Zanzibar! *(She starts to rise, reaching for Pony's hands)*
Come on, jump with me . . .
PONY *(Taking her hands and bouncing)*: This is such a bouncy
bed.
OLIVIA: It was there that he taught me how to live on orchids
and read the stars. . . . Zanzibar, say it!
PONY: Zanzibar! Hey, let's play Geography!

They start jumping together.

OLIVIA: We visited the wonders of the world without taking a
step . . . Baghdad!
PONY: Detroit!
OLIVIA: Vienna!
PONY: Alabama!
OLIVIA: Nicosia . . .
PONY *(Stops jumping)*: No, no you're not playing right. Alabama
ends with A, so you've got to name a place that starts with A!
OLIVIA: Addis Ababa! *(She resumes jumping)*
PONY: That's right! Arizona!
OLIVIA: Athens!
PONY: Sacramento!

They jump higher and higher.

OLIVIA: Oslo!

*Dalia, Charlotte, Wally and Turner come bursting in. They skid to
a stop when they see the two of them bouncing on the bed; Olivia
still in Pony's glasses, Pony, in Olivia's wig.*

DALIA: Señora, Señora . . . ?
PONY: Ohio!
CHARLOTTE: Livvie?!
WALLY: What's happening?
OLIVIA: Odessa!
TURNER: Pony, what have you got on your head?

PONY: We're playing Geography! *(She rips off the wig and flings it in the air)*

OLIVIA: *Odessa!*

PONY: Albuquerque!

CHARLOTTE *(Starts laughing)*: It's a miracle, a miracle!

SYBIL *(Comes streaking in)*: Finally . . .

PONY: *Albuquerque!*

SYBIL *(Laughing)*: You see, you see . . . ?

OLIVIA: Egypt!

SYBIL: What did I tell you!

CHARLOTTE: Look at her go!

WALLY: Unbelievable!

TURNER: She's great, really great!

CHARLOTTE: Go Livvie!

WALLY: Jump!

OLIVIA: I said Egypt! What's the matter with you? Are you deaf?

PONY: Oh, sorry, sorry . . . um . . . Tallahassee!

OLIVIA: Equador!

PONY: Rhode Island!

WALLY: *Jump!*

OLIVIA *(Starts to weaken)*: Denmark.

PONY: Kansas!

OLIVIA *(Weakening more)*: Shanghai!

SYBIL *(Easing Olivia down to the edge of the bed)*: Easy, easy . . .

OLIVIA: I said . . . Shanghai!

PONY: Islip! It's in Long Island.

OLIVIA: Paradise!

PONY: Paradise.

OLIVIA: Come on, say it loud and clear.

PONY: Paradise!

OLIVIA: Again!

PONY *(Bouncing higher)*: Paradise!

OLIVIA: And again!

Pony jumps higher and higher. She starts doing wondrous spins in midair.

PONY: Paradise. . . . Paradise. . . . Paradise!

ALL *(Massing around the bed, overlapping, continuous and euphoric)*: Paradise . . . Paradise . . . Paradise . . . Paradise . . . Paradise . . . Paradise . . . Paradise . . . *(Etc.)*

The light around Pony becomes more intense. Hair flying and nightie billowing, she looks like a reckless angel challenging the limits of heaven.

The curtain slowly falls.

Birth And
After Birth

Characters

SANDY APPLE, a mommy, early 30s
BILL APPLE, her husband, a businessman, middle 30s
NICKY, their 4-year-old son, played by an adult
MIA FREED, an anthropologist, early 30s
JEFFREY FREED, her husband, also an anthropologist, 40s

$\mathcal{A}$ct $\mathcal{O}$ne

The Apple's kitchen, playroom, dining room, living room—a surreal space in which the boundaries between the four rooms have long since collapsed. Sofas and coffee tables coexist with sink, refrigerator and stove. Pots and pans hang next to family photographs and gilt mirrors. A dining room table sits next to a recliner. A TV set is wedged between a dishwasher, toy box and garbage pail. There's even a coat closet in the room. Today is Nicky's fourth birthday. It's early in the morning and still dark. Sandy and Bill are in their bathrobes, racing to get everything ready before Nicky gets up. Bill shakes a tambourine.

SANDY *(Wrapping presents)*: Sssssssssssssshhhhhhhhh!

BILL: God, I love tambourines!

SANDY: You'll wake him up.

BILL: What is it about them?

SANDY: We'll never finish!

BILL: They kill me.

SANDY: Bill!

BILL: If I had my life to live over, I'd be a tambourine virtuoso.

SANDY: I haven't even started wrapping the masks yet.

BILL: Imagine being the greatest tambourine virtuoso in the world . . .

SANDY: At least you got some sleep last night.

BILL: Concerts on every continent: Europe, Australia, South America . . . *(Plays with enthusiasm, doing a few flamenco steps)*

SANDY: There's still the puzzles and coloring books.

NICKY *(Bursting into the room in his pajamas)*: Where's my presents? Where's my presents?

SANDY *(Dropping everything)*: Oh, Nicky, you scared me!

BILL *(Snatching up a video camera)*: Don't do a thing 'til Daddy gets his new video camera!

NICKY *(Tearing through the darkness looking for his presents)*: Where's my presents? Where's my presents?

SANDY: Mommy and Daddy have been up all night getting everything ready for Nicky's party. Does Nicky want to see what they've done? One, two, three! *(She turns on the lights)*

Crepe-paper streamers crisscross the ceiling, balloons hang in clusters, a huge "Happy Birthday" banner is stretched across the room. The table is set for five and seems to float under the weight of favors, candies, noisemakers, and hats. Everything stops; even Nicky is stunned.

BILL *(On top of it all with his camera)*: I'll bet you never expected anything like this, old buddy, did you? Huh? You never dreamed it would be like this!

SANDY *(Throwing her arms around Nicky)*: Just look at you! Mommy's great big four-year-old!

NICKY: Where's my presents? Where's my presents?

BILL: Daddy's present to Nicky is a whole video of Nicky's party.

SANDY: Such a big boy . . . it seems like only yesterday I was bringing him home from the hospital.

NICKY *(Finding his presents and diving into them headfirst)*: Presents! Presents! Oooooooooooooh, look at all my presents!

BILL: Keep it up, Nick, you're doing great, just beautiful . . . beautiful.

SANDY: Nicky, you're not supposed to open presents now. Presents after cards, you know that's the way we do it! *(Starts picking up the shredded wrapping)*

Nicky, ignoring her, tears open musical instruments, plays them.

BILL *(Filming)*: Atta boy, Nick, show 'em how good you can play. Look at Daddy and play something. Over this way . . . look at Daddy!

SANDY: Nicky, I asked you to wait. We do cards first, that way we avoid all this mess at the beginning.

BILL: Oh, Nicholas, are we making one hell of a video!

NICKY: A red wagon! *(Pulling it around the room in rapture)*

BILL: Towards Daddy, honey, come towards Daddy. Oh, Christ, I don't believe this kid.

SANDY *(With a broom)*: Nicky, how is Mommy going to clean all this up? Do you want to have your party inside a great big mess?

BILL: *Stop everything, Nick!* Daddy just got an idea! Let's get some footage of Nicky pulling Mommy in his new red wagon! *(Rushing to Sandy, guiding her into the wagon)* Come on, Mommy, Nicky's going to give you a ride.

SANDY: Hey, what are you doing?

NICKY: Nicky's going to pull his big Mommy present. *(Starts pulling)*

BILL *(Filming)*: Too much. . . . Oh, Jesus. . . . Jesus. . . . Too much!

SANDY *(Dropping her head in her hands)*: Please, Bill, I'm a mess. I haven't even brushed my teeth yet.

NICKY *(Pulling lickety-split)*: Look at Nicky go! Look at Nicky, Daddy. Nicky's pulling his big Mommy present!

SANDY: I've got to clean up.

BILL: Will you look at that kid go?! Don't tell me my son isn't football material!

Nicky pulls Sandy all around the room making hairpin turns. He suddenly sees an unopened present and runs off to it.

BILL: Hey, where are you going? You were doing great!

NICKY: More presents, more, more, *more!*

SANDY: My breath smells.

BILL: Hey, Nick, what the hell? You were pulling Mommy and doing great. Now come back here and pick up that handle!

SANDY: Nobody cares about anything around here.

BILL: I've got an idea. Let's put in some of these presents *with* Mommy! *(Starts piling presents on top of Sandy)*

SANDY: I haven't even had a chance to pee.

NICKY *(Throwing his last opened present across the room)*: Nicky's presents are all gone! *(Starts to cry)*

BILL: Daddy asked you to pick up that wagon handle and pull!

NICKY: I wanted a bunny! And I wanted a puppy . . . and a pony. *Where's my pony?* You said I could get a pony for my birthday!

SANDY *(Combing her hair)*: I stay up all night decorating the room, wrapping the presents, blowing up the balloons, making a really nice party, and what does he do? Just tears into everything. Rips it all up! Ruins everything. *(Gets out of the wagon and sits at the birthday table)*

BILL: All the presents are in the wagon, so get over here, Nicholas and pull! *(Films)*

NICKY *(Kicking the wagon, cries)*: You promised me a pony. *You promised!*

SANDY: And not one thank you. I never heard one thank you for anything.

BILL: I'm waiting!

SANDY: Do you know what my mother would have done if I ruined all my birthday presents and never said thank you?

BILL *(Slamming down his camera)*: Thanks a lot, Nicky. Thanks for ruining a great video!

SANDY: She'd have flushed them down the toilet, that what she would have done!

Nicky gets into the wagon, lies down and sucks his thumb. Bill sits with Sandy at the birthday table.

BILL: Jesus Christ, Nicky.

Silence.

SANDY: He shouldn't be up this early.

BILL: He got up too early.

SANDY *(To Nicky)*: I have a good mind to take you back up to your room!

BILL: If you ask me, he should be sent up to his room!

SANDY: Do you want Daddy to take you up to your room?

BILL: You'd better watch it, young man, or it's up to your room!

SANDY: How would you like to be sent up to your room on your birthday?

Silence.

BILL: He got up too early.

SANDY: Come on, Bill, take him on up.

Silence.

BILL: That kid gets away with murder.

Sandy sighs.

BILL: Absolute murder . . .

Sandy sighs. Silence. Bill imitates Nicky sucking. Sandy sighs.

BILL: He sounds like some . . . sea animal . . . some squid or something. *(Imitates the sound)*

SANDY: All children suck their thumb when they're upset.

BILL *(To Nicky)*: You'll get warts on your tongue if you keep that up!

SANDY: I used to suck mine.

BILL: He'll push his teeth all out of shape.

SANDY *(Popping her thumb into her mouth)*: This one.

BILL: Do you know how much fixing that boy's teeth is going to cost? About three thousand dollars, that's all!

SANDY: I sucked my thumb until I was twenty-two.

BILL: You'll have warts on your tongue and three-thousand-dollar braces on your teeth!

SANDY: I used to suck it during lunch hour when I worked at the insurance company. I'd go into the ladies' room, lock the door, sit on the toilet, and just . . . suck my thumb. *(Laughs)* It sounds ridiculous, a grown woman sucking her thumb on a toilet in the ladies' room.

BILL: Aside from the warts and the three-thousand-dollar braces, it's just so goddamned disgusting! *(Imitates Nicky again)*

SANDY: Come to think of it, I didn't really stop sucking it until Nicky was born.

BILL: In the same category as nose-picking.

SANDY *(Scratching her head)*: It's funny how that sucking instinct gets passed on from the mother to her child.

Silence.

BILL: Four years old. . . . Wow!

SANDY *(Scratching)*: Ever since I got up this morning, I've had this itching . . .

BILL: When a kids turns four, then it's time to buy a video camera, right?

SANDY: It's strange, because I've never had dandruff . . .

BILL: Put away the Super 8 and bring out the camcorder.

SANDY: When I looked I the mirror this morning, I saw an old woman. Not *old* old, just used up. *(She scratches her head; a shower of sand falls out)* It's the weirdest thing, it doesn't look like dandruff or eczema, but more like . . . I don't know, like my head is drying up and leaking . . .

BILL: You see, if Daddy didn't make a video on your birthday, then none of us would remember what you looked like when you were little.

SANDY: My head is leaking . . .

BILL *(Picking up his camera, starts shooting Nicky at close range)*: Time passes so fast, before you know it, you'll be an old man lying in a nursing home.

SANDY *(Shaking out more sand)*: My brains are drying up . . .

BILL: Not a lonely old man, Nick, but one with videos of his youth: birthday parties, Christmases, visits to the zoo.

SANDY *(Pulling out a fistful of hair)*: And now my hair is falling out.

BILL: Shit, you'll be the most popular guy in the nursing home. "Have you seen Mr. Apple's videos of his fourth birthday party?" the little old ladies will say.

SANDY: Poor Mommy's going bald.

BILL: The old people will crowd into your room, blocking the hall with their wheelchairs . . .

SANDY *(Scratching and leaking more sand)*: When she looked in the mirror this morning, she saw an old woman.

BILL: All for that backwards glance at the radiance of youth.

SANDY: Poor old feeble leaking Mommy . . .

BILL: Someday you'll thank me for this.

SANDY: Bald as an egg.

BILL: Come on, give Daddy a big smile now.

NICKY *(Still in the wagon, sucking his thumb)*: I want to make my birthday wish.

BILL *(Holding out a mask for Nicky)*: Hey, Nick, how about putting on this mask?

Sandy sighs.

BILL: Come on, give us a roar.

SANDY: Oh, put on the mask for Daddy!

NICKY: I want to blow out my candles and make my birthday wish.

SANDY: Oh, Nicky, *put it on*!

BILL: I tell you, when we show this movie to the Freeds tonight, they'll eat their hearts out!

SANDY *(Putting the mask on Nicky)*: Look at Nicky!

BILL: Run around the room and pop out from behind the chairs.

NICKY: I don't have to if I don't want to.

BILL: Nicky, I said pop out from behind the chairs! Now, do it!

NICKY: I want raisins.

SANDY: Oooooh, my neck is stiff.

BILL *(Pulling Nicky out of the wagon)*: Move!

NICKY *(Collapsing on the floor)*: Raisins!

BILL: Will you *please* get him to run around the room and pop out from behind the chairs!

SANDY: Come on, Nicky.

NICKY: *Raisins!*

BILL: We're showing the video to the Freeds tonight, so let's get going!

SANDY: That's right. Jeffrey and Mia are coming over to celebrate with us.

BILL: Jeffrey may take good slides, but I promise you he's never seen anything like this!

SANDY: They're bringing you a special present and everything . . .

NICKY: Presents!

SANDY: And you know what great presents Jeffrey and Mia give.

BILL: Nobody gives presents like Jeffrey and Mia. So come on, Nick, pop out from behind the chairs.

SANDY: Remember the Chinese Imperial warrior doll they brought him last year?

NICKY: Presents, presents, presents . . .

SANDY: Jeffrey and Mia are first cousins, honey, Jeffrey and I have the same grandpa.

BILL: *Will you move, goddammit!*

SANDY: I've known Jeffrey ever since he was your age. We used to throw apples on sticks.

BILL: *Nickyyyyyy!*

SANDY: Mommy's planned such a wonderful party with our cousins.

Nothing happens.

BILL *(Lunging at Nicky)*: I said . . . *move!*

Nicky runs around the room, popping up from behind the chairs. Bill can't keep up with him.

BILL: Will you slow down for Christsake?!

Sandy laughs. Nicky stops and flops down inside his wagon.

BILL *(Slamming down his camera)*: Thanks a lot, Nicholas, I'll remember this.

Long silence.

SANDY: My neck is so stiff I can hardly turn my head.

Silence. Bill pulls a letter out of his pocket and sits down.

SANDY: Four years ago Nicky came out of my tummy and made me the happiest mommy in the world.
BILL: I wish you'd look at this letter sometime.

Sandy sighs.

BILL: It came through the office mail last week. I told you about it the other day, remember?
SANDY: I'm a mommy!
BILL: It's from Continental Allied.
SANDY: Who ever thought that I'd be a mommy?
BILL *(Reading)*: "Dear Mr. Apple, It has come to the attention of the accounting department that certain papers in the Fiedler file are either missing or incomplete . . ."
SANDY: Hey, Nicky, I'm a mommy!

Nicky puts on one of his masks. It's the face of a baby. Sandy is enchanted.

SANDY: Oh, Nickyyyyyyyyyy.
BILL: "You assured us last month that the Fiedler account had been settled."
SANDY: Does Nicky want to play Babies?
BILL: "But now it appears there have been certain . . . irregularities . . ."
SANDY: Nicky, we can't play now, Mommy has to get the party ready.

Nicky coos and gurgles inside his mask.

BILL: "Mr. Brill has brought to our attention the outstanding work you did on the Yaddler account . . ."
SANDY: Look at all the mess, honey.

Nicky gurgles louder.

SANDY: Don't you want to have a nice tidy birthday party with everything in its place?

Nicky gets in Sandy's lap, handing her a mask of a pop-eyed Cinderella.

SANDY: Ohhhhhh, Nicky, not now . . .
BILL: "Rest assured, everyone here at Continental Allied knows what a delicate procedure that was . . ."
SANDY *(Putting on the mask)*: Sweet baby.

The game of Babies begins. Nicky is inspired: going limp, gurgling and cooing.

SANDY *(Rocking Nicky)*: Do you know what baby Nicky looked like when he was born, hmmm? *(Kissing him)* A shiny blue fish! Mommy's little blue trout!
BILL: "We are full of admiration for the good judgment you showed on that particular account . . ."
NICKY: I was blue?
SANDY: Of course you were blue. All babies are blue when they're inside their mommies' tummies. It's because there's no air inside the little plastic bag they live in.
NICKY: I want to be blue again. I want to be blue again!
SANDY: Once the baby pops out of the plastic bag, he breathes air for the first time. And do you know what happens to him then?
BILL: "What puzzles us, Mr. Apple, is the professional inconsistency you exhibit in your work . . ."
SANDY: He turns bright pink! As pink as a seashell!

BILL: "Professional inconsistency."

SANDY: Actually, you were a little jaundiced at birth, so your skin was more gold than pink. Mommy's *goldfish*!

NICKY: I was gold?

SANDY: Fourteen-karat gold!

NICKY: Son of a bitch!

SANDY: My Nicky!

BILL: What kind of a phrase is that, "professional inconsistency"?

SANDY: And your little arms were so skinny, they waved every which way. Do you know what baby Nicky's arms looked like?

NICKY: Nicky was such a good baby, all blue and gold inside his plastic bag.

SANDY: French-fried potatoes, that's what they looked like!

Sandy and Nicky laugh.

BILL: *Gibberish!*

SANDY: And Nicky was such a hungry baby! Why, he drank fifteen bottles of sugar water only an hour after he was born!

NICKY: Blue and gold, Nicky was *soooooooo* thirsty! (*Drinking from an imaginary bottle*)

SANDY: The nurses on the floor had never seen anything like it! They stood around my bed and watched you drink one bottle after another: ten, eleven, twelve, thirteen. . . . The head nurse lined up all the empty bottles in a row and took a picture with her camera!

BILL: There's talk around the office that Brill is going to ask for my resignation.

SANDY: Well, after drinking all that sugar water so fast, Nicky's tummy was full of gas bubbles so Mommy had to burp him. (*Starts thumping his back*)

NICKY: Oh, Nicky's tummy full of gas bubbles!

SANDY: So she swatted and pummeled him until Nicky exploded with such a loud burp, he flew across the room and landed in the sink!

BILL: It's quite subtle, don't you think?

NICKY: Baby firsty, baby still firsty!

SANDY: Such a hungry baby!

BILL: And this was over a week ago. *(Pause) You're not even listening to me!* You don't give a good shit if I'm fired! All you care about is playing your moronic baby games with Nicky! *(He storms out of the room)*

Long silence. Sandy takes off her mask.

NICKY: Daddy's mad.

SANDY: Daddy's mad.

Nicky sucks his thumb.

SANDY: Just look at this mess!

NICKY: I don't like it when Daddy's mad.

SANDY: God, Nicky, you have to destroy everything you touch.

NICKY: I want grape juice.

SANDY: I just don't understand you. One minute you're the sweet baby Mommy brought home from the hospital, and the next, you're a savage!

NICKY *(Tearing off his mask)*: I said I want grape juice!

SANDY: We have company coming!

NICKY *(Stamping his foot)*: I want grape juice. I want grape juice. I want grape juice!

SANDY: You don't care if Jeffrey and Mia walk into a shit house! *(Starts cleaning again)*

NICKY: *I'm going to die if I don't have grape juice, and then you'll be sorry!*

SANDY: Well, you can't have grape juice. You'll spoil your appetite for your birthday cake!

NICKY: I want grape juice. I want grape juice. *I want grape juice.*

SANDY *(Cleaning in a fury)*: Mommy said no grape juice.

NICKY *(Hurtling into the middle of her cleaning)*: *Grape juice!*

SANDY *(Shaking him, out of control)*: *Mommy! Said! No!*

Silence. Nicky makes a small strangled sound.

SANDY: Oh, God.

Nicky faints flat on the floor.

SANDY: Oh, God.

Nothing happens.

SANDY: *Billlllll! Nicky's fainted!*

BILL *(Flying into the room)*: What happened? *(He props Nicky up in his arms, and starts walking him)*

SANDY: Oh, Bill, help him. *(Starts to cry)*

BILL: *Quick, the ice!*

SANDY *(Dashing to the refrigerator, takes out the ice, wraps it in a dishtowel and presses it to Nicky's temples)*: It's all right, Nicky, Mommy's got some ice, Mommy will make you all better.

BILL: Come on, Nicker, move those legs of yours! Let's see some action! *(To Sandy) Will you get more ice!*

SANDY *(Trying to force the ice down Nicky's mouth as Bill drags him around the room)*: Open wide, darling, Mommy wants to get some of this nice cold ice against your tongue and cool Nicky off. Open wide . . . poor Nicky, did Mommy get mad and shake her boy?

BILL *(Trying to revive him)*: Keep that circulation going! Keep those veins and arteries open! Come on, Sandy, get the tourniquet for Christsakes!

SANDY *(Running around, panicked)*: Oh, Bill, help him, *help him*! The tourniquet! I forgot the tourniquet! *(Wrapping a dishtowel around his head)*

BILL: *Will you hurry up before he forms a blood clot!*

SANDY: Nicky . . . Nicky . . .

BILL: Come on, we'd better get him over to the sink! *(Dragging Nicky to the sink, turns on the water full blast, shoving his head under it)* That's the boy, let the water splash in your face. Now try and open your mouth and take a deep breath.

SANDY: He isn't moving, Bill, he's still all limp. . . . *Get him to open his eyes at least! I want to see his eyes!*

BILL: *Get me the goddamned flashlight!*

SANDY: Oh, the flashlight . . . how could I have forgotten the flashlight? *(Getting it, shines it in Nicky's eyes)* Oh, Nicky, open your eyes for Mommy. Come on, honey, let Mommy look into your pretty eyes . . .

BILL *(Lays Nicky on the floor and starts giving him artificial respiration. To Sandy)*: Get on his legs, hurry up. *(Chanting)* Up and back, up and back, up and back.

SANDY *(Pumping his legs)*: Maybe he needs more ice. I don't think he got any in his mouth.

BILL AND SANDY *(Faster and faster)*: Breathe. In and out. In and out. In and out.

Their chanting reaches a crescendo. Time passes, Nicky twitches. Sandy and Bill stop, sigh, wait. Silence.

NICKY *(Weakly)*: Sing to me.

SANDY *(Cradling him in her arms)*:
Hush, little baby, don't say a word,
Momma's gonna buy you a mockingbird,
And if that mockingbird don't sing,
Momma's gonna buy you a diamond ring.

Silence.

BILL: We got it in time.

Sandy keeps humming.

BILL: Jesus.

SANDY: What would I do if this ever happened when you weren't here?

BILL: Well, luckily, it only seems to happen when I *am* here.

SANDY: I don't know what I'd do without you.

BILL: *Nick Apple is four years old today!*

NICKY: It hurts being born.

SANDY: I know, honey, I know.

NICKY: It hurts Nicky's head and stomach.

BILL: So tell me, Nick, how does it feel being four? Do you feel any different?

SANDY: "Four" sounds so old.

NICKY: I feel . . . sweeter.

SANDY *(Laughing, hugs him)*: Oh, Nicky.

BILL: And what else?

NICKY: Softer.

BILL: You nut.

NICKY: . . . and cuter.

SANDY: Oh, Nickyyyyy.

NICKY: . . . and furrier!

BILL: Furrier?

NICKY *(Sticking out his hands)*: When I woke up this morning, I saw fur on my hands, white fur.

BILL: *The kid's got fur on his hands!*

SANDY *(Mock-stricken)*: My baby!

BILL *(Grabbing Nicky's arm, inspecting it)*: The kid's got white fur growing up his arm!

NICKY: Nicky's turning into a furry rabbit.

SANDY: Oh, Nicky!

NICKY: I like being a furry rabbit!

SANDY: My baby! What will we do?

NICKY: Look, there's fur on my tongue, too!

BILL: Well, son of a gun!

NICKY: And on my teeth . . .

BILL: We'll have to get carrots and lettuce . . .

SANDY: What will the neighbors say?

BILL *(Whispering)*: They'll never know. . . . We'll keep it a secret.

SANDY: Bill, I'm scared.

NICKY *(Whispering)*: I'll only leave the house at night . . .

BILL: During the day he'll stay in his room . . .

NICKY: I'll hide under my bed.

BILL: We'll build vast underground tunnels . . . no one will suspect a thing . . .

NICKY: By day I'll hide under my bed eating carrots, and at night I'll roam the countryside.

SANDY: Ooooooh, Nicky!

BILL: For long periods of time he'll disappear altogether.

NICKY: I'll be known as . . . Rabbit Boy.

BILL: He'll become a champion of rabbits in distress.

NICKY: I'll learn rabbit magic.

BILL: He'll cast spells. He'll turn buildings into giant carrots!

NICKY: *Let's play Rabbit Says.*

SANDY: Oh, Nicky, not now.

NICKY *(Standing on a chair)*: Rabbit says, "Raise your hands!"

BILL: Later, Nick.

SANDY: Please, honey.

NICKY: Rabbit says, "Raise your hands!"

BILL: We have the whole rest of the day.

NICKY: Rabbit says, "Raise your hands!"

Sandy and Bill raise their hands.

NICKY: Rabbit says, "Scratch your nose."

Sandy and Bill scratch their noses.

NICKY: Rabbit says, "Lift your right leg."

Sandy and Bill do everything he says.

NICKY: Rabbit says, "Lift your left leg." Rabbit says, "Stick out your tongue." *Reach for the sky! (Nicky laughs, clapping his hands)* I tricked you, I tricked you! Rabbit says, "Rub your belly." Rabbit says, "Hop on two feet." *Hop on one foot!*

Sandy and Bill blindly obey.

NICKY: You did it! You did it! *(Going faster)* Rabbit says, "Lie on the floor." Rabbit says, "Get up." Rabbit says, "Fart."

Bill makes a farting noise in his armpit.

SANDY: Not this again!
NICKY: Rabbit says, "Fart again."

Bill does.

SANDY: I'm not playing, it's disgusting.
NICKY: Rabbit says, "Fart three times in a row."

Bill does.

SANDY: It isn't funny, Nicholas!
NICKY: Rabbit says, "Run after Nicky and play Fart Tag."

Bill chases Nicky, making a farting sound every time he tags him.

SANDY: If this is the only way you can celebrate Nicky's birthday, it's just pathetic! *(Sits down and stares into space)*

Bill and Nicky keep playing.

SANDY: My front teeth feel loose . . . *(Leaning over, shakes a
shower of sand from her hair)* It's the strangest thing—I've been
smelling the sea all morning. We're hundreds of miles away
from it, but that bitter salty smell of low tide is unmistakable. I
noticed it the moment the sun came up. *(Inhales, shaking out
more sand)* Nicky, I'd like you to come back to the table and
open your cards.
BILL *(Sits Nicky in his lap, rumpling his hair)*: Nicky's four!
NICKY: I love you, Daddy.
SANDY: He got more cards than he did last year.

Bill starts tickling Nicky.

NICKY *(Laughing)*: Don't!

SANDY *(Opening a card, reads)*:
"This little pony comes galloping by,
With a smile on his face and a gleam in his eye.
Seems it's somebody's birthday, 'neigh, neigh, neigh,'
Somebody special who's four today!"
From Walt and Sally, and look, they sent five dollars.

BILL *(Still tickling Nicky)*: Is Nicky ticklish?

NICKY *(Screaming with pleasure)*: Stop . . . Stop!

SANDY *(Reading another card)*:
"May God in his glory look down from the sky,
With a birthday blessing for a wonderful guy."
The Blys. How thoughtful.

BILL: I tell you, Nick, we're going to have a great party tonight!

SANDY: Will you look at this! Nicky got a card from Mrs. Tanner, his nursery school teacher, and they have a strict policy of not sending individual cards on the children's birthdays. *(In a singsong)* I guess someone is Mrs. Tanner's favorite! *(Long pause)* It's important for a child to form attachments outside the home.

BILL *(With Nicky on his lap)*: Children need guidelines!

SANDY: An ounce of prevention is worth a pound of cure.

BILL: If a child isn't given boundaries, he'll be emotionally crippled for life!

SANDY: *I* believe in discipline!

BILL: Children learn from observation!

SANDY: Tolerance comes from awareness.

BILL: Self-respect is built on sharing!

SANDY: Reading readiness precedes cognition!

BILL: If I ever caught Nicky with matches, right out! I'd toss him right out of the house!

Silence.

SANDY: I feel sorry for Jeffrey and Mia. I wish there was something we could do.

BILL: It's none of our business.

SANDY: But not to have children . . .

BILL: You can't run other people's lives.

SANDY: *Neither* of them wants children!

BILL: Their careers are very important to them.

NICKY: I love birthdays!

SANDY: But they're missing so much.

NICKY: What I love most is blowing out the candles and making my wish.

SANDY: What if they changed their minds tonight . . .

NICKY: Sally told me all birthday wishes come true.

SANDY: What if they finally decided to have a baby?

BILL: Jeffrey and Mia have been married for twelve years. I don't think they're suddenly going to change their minds at Nicky's party.

SANDY: But what if they did?

NICKY: I know just the wish I'm going to make!

BILL: It won't happen.

SANDY: But what if they just . . . did . . . because of us and Nicky and how happy we all are.

NICKY: And it's going to come true because Sally said so.

SANDY: Oh, Bill, I bet they change their minds tonight, just wait and see!

BILL: What's going to happen tonight is that we're going to have one hell of a party for Nicky, and I'm going to show one hell of a video!

SANDY: I have a feeling . . .

NICKY: When can I blow out the candles and make my wish?

SANDY: Imagine being a woman and not wanting to experience birth.

BILL: People are different.

SANDY: But never to have your own baby . . .

NICKY: When can I blow out the candles and make my wish?

SANDY: It would be so good for both of them.

BILL: As anthropologists studying children of primitive cultures, they see a lot of suffering.

NICKY: I want to make my birthday wish.

BILL: Once you've seen children dying of starvation, I'm sure you think twice about bringing more people into the world.

SANDY: But their baby wouldn't starve!

NICKY: I want to make my birthday wish!

SANDY: They'd have such a beautiful baby.

BILL: They're not interested in having a beautiful baby, they're interested in studying primitive children!

NICKY: Mommy, can I make my birthday wish now?

SANDY: *No, you cannot make your wish now, Mommy's talking to Daddy and it's very important. (Pause)* How can they understand primitive children if they don't have children of their own?

BILL: Just because I can articulate their reasons for not wanting children doesn't mean I agree with them!

NICKY: Daddy, can I make my birthday wish now?

SANDY: Well, you don't have to be so pompous about it. People do change!

BILL: It's very unlikely.

SANDY: But it could happen . . .

BILL: Well, anything *could* happen, but that doesn't mean . . .

NICKY: Please, Daddy, can I make my . . .

SANDY: *Shit, Nicky, can't you let Mommy and Daddy have a conversation?!*

BILL: Mommy and Daddy are talking now.

NICKY *(Starting to cry)*: It's not fair . . . it's not fair . . .

SANDY: He's impossible!

BILL: Can't you just wait . . .

Nicky cries louder.

SANDY: Keep this up, Nicky, and there won't *be* any birthday party!

NICKY: Go on, yell at me and be mean, I don't care because I still haven't made my birthday wish and when I make it, it will come true because Sally said so!

He exits. Long silence.

SANDY *(Glancing at herself in the mirror)*: When I looked in the mirror this morning, I saw an old woman. Not *old* old, just used up. *(Takes off her slipper and dumps out a stream of sand)*

BILL: Kids!

SANDY *(Sighs)*: I don't know.

Silence.

BILL *(Holding up a party favor)*: Remember those surprise balls we used to get at parties when we were kids? Those endless ribbons of crepe paper rolled up with little metal toys inside?

SANDY: He has such a temper.

BILL: It's funny, you never see them around anymore. *(Pause)* We had some birthday parties in those days! One birthday I'll never forget, and that was my eleventh! *Shit, what a party!*

SANDY: My eighth was the best. I invited the entire class. It was on a Saturday afternoon and we strung white streamers from one end of the dining room to the other.

BILL: My mother let me invite the whole class. Thirty-three kids came!

SANDY: All the girls got pincushions for favors, and the boys got yo-yos that glowed in the dark. And instead of having cake and ice cream, my mother made this incredible baked Alaska.

BILL: We decorated the whole place in red: red streamers, red balloons, red tablecloth . . .

SANDY: When she brought it to the table, everyone gasped. It was three feet high and covered with peaks of egg white.

BILL: Shit, everything was red! My mother even put red food coloring in the cake.

SANDY: I can still remember the taste . . . like sweetened snow.

BILL: That was the birthday I got my red bike. And when we'd finished eating the red cake and red raspberry ice cream, we played games.

SANDY: I don't know where we got the room, but we actually set up twenty-seven chairs for musical chairs.

BILL: Darts, ducking for apples . . .

SANDY: We played it once, then twice.

BILL: Then we set up chairs and played musical chairs.

SANDY: By the fifth round we decided to alter the rules a little . . .

BILL: But after a while we changed the rules.

SANDY: When you sat down in a chair, you grabbed someone of the opposite sex and they sat in your lap.

BILL: It was getting boring with the same old rules.

SANDY: . . . and then you had to . . . had to . . .

BILL: So you grabbed a girl and both sat on the chair together.

SANDY: . . . you had to . . . had to . . .

BILL: And you kissed the girl for as long as you could without coming up for air, and whoever kissed the longest played in the next round.

SANDY: We played musical chairs.

BILL: After the kissing part, we began unbuttoning the girls' blouses and putting our hands inside. *(Pulling Sandy onto his lap)*

SANDY: We played it once, twice, then three times.

BILL *(Nuzzling her)*: And feeling what there was to feel. Oh, it was nice, it was very nice.

SANDY: By the fifth round we decided to alter the rules a little.

BILL *(His hands in her robe)*: And each time the music stopped, you grabbed another girl and reached down into another blouse . . .

SANDY: When you sat down in a chair, you grabbed someone of the opposite sex and he sat in your lap.

BILL: After a while we forgot all about the musical part of the game and everyone was just lying all over the chairs, kissing and feeling up.

SANDY: I don't know why the grownups didn't . . .

BILL *(Caressing Sandy)*: Some of us even got our pants off.

SANDY *(Laughing)*: Bill!

BILL *(More and more amorous)*: We locked the door and pulled down the shades.

SANDY: Someone might come in.

BILL: Tommy Hartland and I got five girls under the table.

SANDY *(Resisting)*: Oh, Bill.

BILL: But by the time we got our Jockeys off, the girls panicked and were back in the game with someone else, and there were

Tommy Hartland and I, horny as hell, surrounded by all these goddamned red streamers and strawberry gumdrops.

SANDY: I remember, my mother made this baked Alaska. It was covered with egg whites . . .

BILL: Come on, give us a kiss.

SANDY: Don't, Nicky might come in . . .

BILL: Nicky's not coming in, just relax.

SANDY: Please, Bill, not now, I just can't . . . Nicky . . .

They struggle. Nicky bursts into the room, dressed up in Sandy's underwear. A slip trails on the ground, a bra is draped around his waist, a stocking hangs from his neck He's stricken with jealousy.

NICKY:	SANDY *(Flying off*	BILL:
Mommy!	*Bill's lap)*:	*You little prick!*
	Nicky!	

NICKY: *I want grape juice!*

BILL: *What in hell are you doing in your mother's underwear?*

SANDY: That's a seventy-five dollar bra you've got wrapped around your waist.

BILL: I never even *dreamed* of going through my mother's underwear!

NICKY: *I want grape juice! I want grape juice!*

SANDY: I don't believe it.

BILL: That child should be punished.

NICKY *(Louder still)*: *And I . . . want . . . ice . . . in . . . my . . . grape . . . juice!*

BILL: Well, you can't have ice in your grape juice, you little—

SANDY *(Shoving a glass of grape juice at Nicky)*: Here's your damned grape juice, without ice . . . nice and *warm!*

NICKY *(Hurling the glass to the floor)*: Then I won't drink it!

SANDY *(Rushing to her broom)*: *Look out, broken glass!*

BILL: Did you see what he just did? He deliberately threw his glass on the floor!

NICKY *(Lunging towards it)*: *I want to make my birthday wish! I want to make my birthday wish!*

BILL *(Pulling him back)*: *Mommy said look out!*

NICKY *(Starting to cry)*: Daddy hurt me, Daddy hurt me.

SANDY *(Sweeping)*: It's all over the floor. Don't anybody go near there until I clean it up!

BILL: I didn't hurt him, For Chrissake, I was just trying to keep him away from the glass!

NICKY: *You did so hurt me, you stupid idiot!* (Kicks Bill in the shins)

BILL *(Shaking Nicky with each word)*: Don't . . . you . . . ever . . . hit . . . your . . . father!

Nicky wails.

BILL: Did you see that? Your son just kicked me in the shin. *(Examines the wound)*

SANDY *(Sweeping)*: If you ever deliberately break a glass like that again, I'll . . .

BILL: He broke the skin . . .

SANDY: I've had enough. Take him up to his room, there'll be no party!

BILL: My own son drew blood.

SANDY: I'll phone Jeffrey and Mia and tell them to forget the whole thing.

BILL: You'd better get the peroxide to sterilize it with.

Nicky lies down in his wagon and makes his strangled sound.

SANDY: Come on, Bill, take him up to his room. We're calling the party off.

NICKY: But what about my cake?

SANDY: No birthday party for Nicky this year.

NICKY: . . . and the candles?

BILL: You can spend the rest of the day up in your room.

NICKY: What about my wish? *(Starts to cry)*

SANDY: The child has to be punished.

BILL: It's your own fault, Nicky, we gave you every chance.

NICKY: You mean I won't have any party at all?

SANDY: We warned you.

BILL: It hurts us more than it does you.

SANDY: *You've got to learn some time, Nicholas!*

BILL: Maybe next year you'll be a better boy.

SANDY: *I asked you to wait and open your presents after the cards!*

NICKY: No party? No wish?

BILL: We certainly don't enjoy doing this, Nicky.

SANDY: No party, and that's that.

Nicky runs out of the room crying.

SANDY: I'm sorry, Nicky.

BILL: We gave you every chance.

SANDY: We gave him every chance.

The curtain slowly falls.

Act Two

Around six-thirty that evening. Sandy, Bill and Nicky sit around the birthday table dressed in party clothes. They wear paper hats and are making barnyard sounds. Sandy clucks like a chicken, Bill howls like a coyote and Nicky oinks like a pig.

BILL: One, two, three—change!

Sandy meows, Bill grunts like a gorilla, Nicky barks.

BILL: One, two, three—change!

Sandy whinnies, Bill whistles like a thrush, Nicky bleats like a goat.

BILL: One, two, three—change!

Sandy clucks like a chicken, Bill croaks like a frog, Nicky hoots like an owl.

BILL: Stop! Mommy's out of the game! She already clucked before!

Bill roars like a lion; Nicky makes fish noises and faces.

BILL *(Faster)*: One, two, three—change!

Bill hisses like a snake; Nicky gobbles like a turkey.

BILL: One, two, three—change!

Bill grunts like a gorilla; Nicky squeaks like a mouse.

BILL: Stop the game! Daddy already made gorilla grunts before, Nicky wins!

BILL AND SANDY *(Applauding and whistling)*: Yea, Nicky, yea, Nicky!

NICKY: Let's play again.

SANDY: You're too good for us.

NICKY: Let's play again.

SANDY: They should be here any time now.

BILL: Is everybody ready for one hell of a party?

SANDY: Oh, Nicky, I can hardly wait!

BILL: They will eat their hearts out when they see this video!

SANDY: The whole day would be perfect if only Jeffrey and Mia changed their minds about having children. Tonight, with us.

BILL: I've always admired Jeffrey as a photographer, but frankly I think he overrates himself.

Nicky runs around the room making animal sounds.

SANDY: They may have exciting careers now, but what about when they're retired and all alone in the world.

BILL: Just because he does a lot of traveling he fancies himself a professional photographer!

NICKY *(Braying in their ears)*: Let's play again.

SANDY: If she waits much longer, it will be too late. Remember Diane Oak? Diane Oak waited until she was forty-five before she had Jonathan. Her cervix had shriveled up by then and wouldn't even open for the birth.

NICKY: What's a cervix?

SANDY: She passed her ninth month, tenth, eleventh, twelfth . . . nothing happened. They finally had to induce her in her fifteenth.

NICKY: What's a cervix?
SANDY: When that poor baby was finally pulled out by Cesarean section, he weighed thirty-six pounds and had a full set of teeth.
NICKY: What's a cervix?
BILL: It's a part of a lady.
NICKY: What part?
SANDY: The part the baby comes out of, sweetheart.
BILL *(Whispering)*: The hole.
NICKY: The poopie hole?
BILL: Not the poopie hole! The baby hole!
NICKY: Where's the baby hole?

Bill indicates on himself where it is.

SANDY: I certainly wouldn't want Mia to go through what Diane Oak did. All her female plumbing was ripped to shreds by that child.
BILL: Babies come out of the baby hole and poopie comes out of the poopie hole.
SANDY: Of course they could always adopt, but it just isn't the same.
NICKY: Where's the poopie hole?

Bill indicates on himself where it is.

SANDY: How she and Jeffrey can call themselves authorities on children when they've never had one of their own . . .
NICKY: Does Mia have a baby hole?
SANDY: She's never felt life moving inside her. It's so sad.
BILL: Of course Mia has a baby hole. All women have baby holes.
NICKY: Then why doesn't a baby come out of it?
SANDY: Of course we don't get to travel like they do, we don't have their kind of freedom . . .
NICKY: Why doesn't a baby come out of Mia's baby hole?

SANDY: . . . and we don't speak all the languages they do.

BILL: Maybe there is one in there, but it's stuck.

NICKY *(Laughing)*: Stuck in with the poopie.

SANDY: They get out more than we do.

NICKY: How does a lady tell whether she's going to have a baby or a poopie?

SANDY: Of course Mia looks younger than me . . .

BILL: Because if it's a baby inside her, her tummy swells up, and if it's a poopie inside her . . .

SANDY: She's missing the most basic experience a woman can have, and when you come right down to it, all she's left with are memories of other people's children.

NICKY: Why doesn't a baby come out of Mia's baby hole?

SANDY: Tape recordings and photographs of strangers . . .

BILL: Because she doesn't want it to.

SANDY: Slides of foreign urchins eating raw elephant meat. I feel sorry for her.

BILL: We all have different needs.

SANDY *(Getting louder)*: It's pathetic. Trying to have her own family through other people's children, and not even American children but poor starving—

The doorbell rings.

BILL AND SANDY: They're here.

SANDY *(Whispering)*: Oh, God, they heard us!

BILL *(Whispering)*: Don't be silly, they couldn't possibly have heard us.

SANDY *(Head in hands)*: They heard us.

BILL *(Going to the door)*: They didn't hear us.

SANDY: They heard us.

NICKY: *Heard what?*

SANDY: *Sssssshhhhhhhh!*

Bill opens the door; Mia and Jeffrey enter, out of breath. Jeffrey is professorial, Mia is a fragile beauty.

JEFFREY	MIA	SANDY	BILL
(Shaking hands with Bill): I'm sorry we're so late. Mia was delivering a paper at an anthropology convention and got tied up with a lot of questions at the end. *(Kissing Sandy)* Sandy, I'm sorry. *(Sets down a slide projector, screen and several boxes of slides)*	*(Kissing Bill)*: Bill, forgive us. I was giving a paper at a convention and some visiting professors from Manila had all these questions . . . *(Kissing Sandy)* Sandy, we finally made it!	*(Kissing both Jeffrey and Mia)*: Jeffrey! Mia! It's so good to see you. Come in, please . . .	*(Slapping Jeffrey on the back)*: We were beginning to worry about you. Come in . . .

Silence, then:

| BILL *(Kissing Mia)*: Mia, you look beautiful, as always. Come in! | MIA *(Kissing Nicky)*: Nicky, four years old! | JEFFREY *(Shaking hands with Nicky)*: Happy birthday, Nicky. | NICKY: I'm four today. Four! |

BILL *(Leading them into the room)*: Come on in.

SANDY: We were beginning to worry . . .

MIA: Oh, Sandy, look at what you've done!

Silence, then:

| BILL: Well folks, everybody ready for a great party? | SANDY: Nicky's been so excited . . . | MIA: Jeffrey, look what they've done! |

They laugh, then silence.

BILL: There's nothing like a kid's fourth birthday!

MIA: We'll give Nicky his present at the table with the cake and ice cream.

They laugh, silence.

SANDY: It just wouldn't have been a real celebration without you!

NICKY: I got a wagon and masks.

BILL: . . . and wait till you see the video we made . . .

They laugh, silence.

JEFFREY: When the Tunisian hill child turns four, he's blindfolded and led into a swamp to bring back the body of a mud turtle for a tribal feast.
SANDY: How fascinating.
MIA: If he fails, he's expelled from the tribe.
JEFFREY: And left on the plains to be picked apart by giant caw-caws.
SANDY: How horrifying!

Silence.

MIA: In the Tabu culture, four is believed to be a magical age. I once saw a four-year-old Tabu girl skin a sixteen-hundred-pound zebra and then eat the pelt!
BILL: Son of a bitch!
NICKY: I can write my name.
MIA: How wonderful.
JEFFREY: I saw the same child nurse a dead goat back to life.
BILL: Jesus!
JEFFREY: With her own milk!
NICKY: I pulled Mommy in my wagon.
MIA: How wonderful.

SANDY: Come, let's sit down around the table.

MIA: Sandy, everything is just . . . beautiful!

JEFFREY: It's really amazing what you can do to a room with some crepe paper and a little imagination.

NICKY *(To Mia)*: Do you have a baby hole?

SANDY: *Nicky!*

BILL: Nicky and I made a great video this morning, didn't we, Nick?

NICKY: Daddy and I made a video.

MIA: How wonderful.

SANDY: Bill and Nicky are very close. They've always been close. Ever since Nicky was born they were close.

NICKY *(To Mia)*: Do you have a baby hole?

SANDY *(Fast)*: It's really quite unusual to find a father and son who are as close as Bill and Nicky.

BILL: I wasn't at all close to my father.

SANDY: I was very close to my father.

MIA: I was close to my mother.

SANDY: I hated my mother.

BILL: I don't remember my mother.

JEFFREY: My mother and father were very close.

BILL: That's interesting, because my mother and father weren't close at all.

Silence.

MIA: Sandy, this room is a work of art! I've never seen anything like it.

SANDY: Well, how often does your favorite son turn four?

NICKY: I got lots of presents.

MIA: You must have been up all night.

NICKY: I got a wagon.

MIA: I'll bet you did!

SANDY: . . . *and* birthday cards. Nicky got twenty-seven birthday cards this year, including one from Mrs. Tanner, his nursery school teacher. And they have a strict policy of not sending individual cards on the children's birthdays. You know, they

might forget somebody. So naturally Nicky was thrilled . . . I
mean, to be singled out like that . . . *(Hands Mia the card)*

MIA *(Reading)*: "Happy birthday, Nicky. Sincerely, Mrs. Tanner."

SANDY *(To Nicky)*: Mrs. Tanner sent that especially to you,
breaking all the school rules!

MIA *(Examining the card)*: That's funny, this looks like your
handwriting.

SANDY: So, cousins, how long will you be with us before you
disappear over the horizon again on the back of some camel?

MIA: Her Y's and N's are exactly like yours.

SANDY *(Snatching the card away)*: People will start thinking you
don't like American children, the way you're always running off
to interview toddlers in Iceland and Nigeria.

NICKY: I pulled Mommy in my wagon.

BILL: He's very strong for his age.

JEFFREY: One of the interesting things about the Berbers is
that parents regard spiritual strength much more highly than
physical strength.

NICKY: I pulled Mommy and all my presents too!

MIA: Almost any Berber child can converse with desert vegeta-
tion.

SANDY: Really?

JEFFREY: To my mind, there are no children the equal of
Berber children!

NICKY: I got instruments for my birthday.

MIA: That's wonderful, Nicky.

SANDY: I know we spoil him, but we just can't help it.

BILL: We spoil the living crap out of that kid and we love every
minute of it, right, Nick?

NICKY: Daddy made a video of me.

SANDY: Bill and Nicky are very close.

NICKY *(Putting on a mask)*: I got masks for my birthday.

SANDY: Nicky and his masks . . .

BILL: Give that kid a mask, any kind of mask, and he's in
seventh heaven!

MIA: We've always been fascinated by masks and the whole
phenomenon of taking on the identity of someone else.

Nicky runs around the room, grunting.

JEFFREY: Remember those crocodile masks we were given in
New Guinea?
SANDY: He gets so excited on his birthday.
BILL: He's been up since six this morning.
JEFFREY: Mia and I were given crocodile masks in New Guinea
that were made out of a paste of dried insects.
MIA: You had the feeling that if you left one on too long, your
face would slowly blend into it and lose all human features.
SANDY: Uuuuuugh.
BILL: Nicky has an unusually vivid imagination.
SANDY: You should hear his dreams . . .
BILL: All about man-eating chairs and flying dogs.
SANDY: Really wild!

Nicky makes more and more noise running around the room.

SANDY: *All right, Nicky, that's enough!*
BILL: Come on, Nick, quiet down.
SANDY: He's been up since five-thirty this morning.
BILL *(Chasing Nicky)*: Okay, Nicky, let's take off the mask and
calm down.
NICKY: *I don't want to take off my mask!*
BILL *(Wresting it away after finally catching him)*: You're being
too wild!
NICKY *(Wailing)*: I want my mask, I want my mask!
SANDY: Let him keep it on. Poor thing, he's exhausted. He was
up at four-thirty this morning.
BILL: Okay, okay, you can have your mask back, but no more
being wild . . . *understand?*

*Nicky puts the mask back on, sits in his chair and sucks his thumb
through the mask. Silence.*

BILL *(Whispering)*: Take your thumb out of your mask.

Nicky doesn't.

SANDY: It's the strangest thing, but ever since I got up this morning I've been smelling the sea. *(Runs her hands through her hair, a shower of sand falls out)*

Silence.

BILL: Tell us again, just how many languages can the two of you speak?

JEFFREY: Seventeen.   MIA: Thirteen.

SANDY: *Jeffrey and Mia can speak fifteen languages, Nicky.*

BILL: My maternal grandmother was Canadian and always spoke French around the house.

SANDY: My maternal grandmother was Dutch.

BILL: But us kids never learned it.

JEFFREY: Canadian French isn't considered a pure language, it's a dilution.

SANDY: I'm part Dutch on one side and Swedish on the other.

BILL: I'm pure Canadian and a little Irish.

NICKY: What am I?

BILL: No, wait, I forgot, I have some Greek blood in me too.

SANDY: Oh, Mia, say a few words in something for Nicky.

NICKY: What am I?

SANDY: Mia's going to say something in a funny language, honey.

NICKY *(Insistent)*: What am I?

BILL *(Angry)*: *Canadian, Dutch, Swedish, and a little Greek!*

Silence.

MIA: Talla zoo zoo feeple zip.

NICKY *(Laughing)*: What did you say?

SANDY *(Laughing)*: Isn't it a riot?

BILL *(Laughing)*: Jesus Christ!

NICKY: What did you say?

MIA: *Happy birthday!*

NICKY: Say something else.
SANDY: Oh, say more!
MIA: Dun herp zala zala cree droop soy nitch.
SANDY *(Roaring with laughter)*: Stop, stop!
NICKY: Say it again, say it again!
BILL: Oh, God!
MIA: Dun herp zala zala cree droop soy nitch.
BILL: What . . . what was it?
MIA: *Merry Christmas!*

Sandy, Bill and Nicky howl with laughter.

SANDY: That was Merry Christmas?
NICKY: Say, "Nicky is four years old today."
MIA: Ooola oola zim dam zilco reet treet comp *graaaaa, Nicky!*

The Apples laugh.

SANDY AND NICKY: Again, again!
MIA AND JEFFREY: Ooola oola zim dam zilco reet treet comp *graaaaa, Nicky!*

All laugh.

BILL *(To Nicky)*: How would you like to be able to speak like that?
NICKY *(Gravely)*: Lim biddle ree yok slow iffle snee buddle twee rat ith twank.
MIA: Nice . . . very nice.
BILL AND SANDY *(Laughing)*: Oh, Nicky, Nicky.
SANDY: We always have such a good time when you two come over!
MIA: We wouldn't miss Nicky's birthday for the world.
SANDY: Who else has cousins that speak fifteen languages?
BILL: Hey, I haven't told Jeffrey and Mia about Charley E.Z., this crazy guy that works in our office.
SANDY: He made the whole thing up.

BILL: There's a shakedown going on at the office, and several of the top-level guys are being let go. And the things they do to try and hang on. Unbelievable. I guess something comes over a guy when he feels his job threatened . . .

SANDY: Bill, really, I . . .

BILL: There's this guy Charles E. Zinn—Charley E.Z., we call him. He's a junior officer who recently lost an important account, so word came down that Charley E.Z. was going to be axed.

JEFFREY: I don't think I've ever heard you mention a Charley E.Z. before.

SANDY: He made it all up.

BILL: He'd been getting these letters accusing him of "professional inconsistency." Have you ever heard such a phrase—"professional inconsistency"?

MIA: I have a feeling this is going to be another of Bill's wild stories.

BILL: So the word came down that Charley E.Z. was going to lose his job.

JEFFREY: Oh, no!

MIA: How awful!

JEFFREY: Poor guy.

BILL: So Charley E.Z. took action. And where did he take action? In the elevator! *(Lowering his voice)* For the past few months between three and four in the afternoon Charley has been getting into the elevator and taking off his clothes, starting with his jacket, shirt, then pants, socks, shoes, and underwear. But the first time he did it, it was cold turkey.

Nicky disappears into the hall closet. He opens the door after several moments, dressed only in his underwear. He mimes "Charley E.Z." opening and shutting the door as Bill tells his story.

BILL: He changed in the executive men's room, stuffed his clothes in a duffel bag, glided into the hall when no one was looking, rang for the elevator, stepped in . . . and began his long, lonely, naked journey.

SANDY *(Laughing)*: Oh, Bill!

BILL: You see, there's a special control panel in the elevator that lets the operator open and shut the door whenever he wants. So if Charley E.Z. is cruising around between the seventeenth and eighteenth floors, say, and someone rings on Main and the door starts to open, and Charley sees someone he doesn't know, he just zaps the close-door button, the door slams shut and Charley zooms back up, safe with his secret.

SANDY *(Laughing, to Mia)*: Isn't he crazy?

MIA *(Laughing)*: Completely . . .

BILL: *Charley's first day in the elevator.* He's in there, cold turkey, nothing on, not even a cuff link. The bell rings on twenty-one. Charley braces himself. The elevator rises. Stops. The door opens and in steps this account executive. He doesn't notice anything. Charley's cool, but by the time they're between eight and nine he looks at Charley. No one says a word. Charley lets him off at Main. One minute later, he gets another call. Guess who?

ALL: The account executive!

BILL: *The account executive!* Well, for the rest of the afternoon the two of them just kept riding up and down, down and up. One of the secretaries on twelve said when the elevator stopped at her floor she caught a fleeting glimpse of two naked men rolling around on the floor, laughing.

MIA: Amazing . . .

BILL: Lately he's taken to props: disguises, musical instruments, special effects.

Nicky opens and shuts the closet door, wearing a variety of masks.

BILL: Last week he was in there with a viola and the entire accounting department.

SANDY: And they all take their clothes off?

BILL: Take them off and throw them down the elevator shaft.

SANDY: Imagine businessmen doing that!

MIA: I never realized there was such an allure for the forbidden in business.

BILL *(Whispering)*: I've heard that next week he's hiring a string trio to play Schubert in the service elevator.

SANDY: Bill made a wonderful video of Nicky opening his presents this morning.

BILL: The point is that everybody at Continental Allied loves Charley E.Z. now. The letters about "professional inconsistency" have slowed to a trickle and he's doing just great.

Silence.

MIA: Don't you think it's time we gave Nicky his present, Jeffrey?

NICKY *(Opening the closet door)*: Up, please. Elevator going up. Please move to the rear of the car to make room for the people getting on. *(Slams the door)*

SANDY *(Knocking on the door)*: Jeffrey and Mia want to give you your present now, honey.

JEFFREY *(Puttering with his slides and projector)*: Nicholas, you've never gotten a present like this! *(Start setting up his equipment)*

SANDY: Presents!

MIA: I just hope he likes it, you never know with children. But we put a great deal of thought into it.

SANDY: Nicky . . .

NICKY *(Opening the door)*: Top floor, everybody off. *(Slams the door)*

SANDY *(Lowering her voice)*: Please, Nicky, you're embarrassing us. It's the strangest thing, but one of my front teeth is loose. People don't lose their front teeth, do they?

MIA: The Qua tribe starts out with all their permanent teeth and then at the age of sixteen every one falls out to be replaced with an entire new set of baby teeth. It's a complete mystery to dental science.

SANDY: How disgusting.

MIA: We were taping interviews with Qua mothers a few months ago. Wonderful people: highly resourceful. They used to prepare these aromatic banquets for us out of tree bark.

SANDY: Uuuuugh! I could never eat that native food. It always looks like human excrement.

MIA: Qua *women* have no teeth at all.

JEFFREY: They eat by grinding their food into a paste between large stones and then lapping it up.

SANDY: Uuuuuuugh!

JEFFREY: Okay, folks, we're ready to go. Get Nicky, his present is all set.

SANDY: He's always so thrilled to see you!

BILL: *Come out, come out, wherever you are!*

SANDY: Family means so much to him.

JEFFREY *(Dimming the lights)*: The show is about to begin.

SANDY: Oooooh, Nicky, I wonder what it is!

BILL *(Opening the closet door)*: *Nicholas, will you get the hell out of there!*

SANDY: You're being very rude, Nicky, Mommy isn't going to forget this.

BILL *(Dragging Nicky out of the closet, now dressed)*: *Now come over here and sit down!*

Bill sits Nicky down. The birthday chairs have been rearranged to face the movie screen. A silence.

JEFFREY *(Rises, waves his hand over the slide projector and box of slides)*: Happy birthday, Nicky.

MIA: Happy birthday.

NICKY: What is it?

JEFFREY: Your own projector with slides of children from all over the world.

Jeffrey starts showing slides of children in native dress doing all kinds of remarkable things. Every few seconds a new picture is flashed on the screen.

SANDY: Oooooooooh, Nicky!

BILL: What a present!

SANDY: Oooooooooooh, Nicky, look!

MIA: We took them all.

SANDY: They're just beautiful.

BILL: Son of a bitch!

JEFFREY: We figured this would be something he could work himself.

MIA: And learn from.

BILL: I've never seen such clarity of color. What kind of film were you using?

SANDY: And Jeffrey and Mia said you could keep them!

NICKY: Isn't there anything else?

BILL: Shit! That's color!

NICKY: . . . something to unwrap?

JEFFREY: All you do is load the projector and then push this button when you want to see a new slide. Your mommy and daddy can help you with it.

NICKY: This is it?

MIA: These are some of the children we worked with last year.

SANDY: Jeffrey and Mia lead very special lives, honey, they travel all over the world studying poor children.

JEFFREY: Oh, look! The Io children. They decorate their faces with an iridescent paint made out of powdered giraffe hooves.

MIA: It's very bad for their skin, actually.

SANDY: I can imagine.

MIA: They're wonderful children. Highly motivated. Jeffrey and I got very close to them.

NICKY: I wish I could meet them.

MIA: Well, maybe someday, Nicky.

NICKY: I wish I could play with them. I don't have anybody to play with.

SANDY: That isn't true. You have Daddy and me to play with, and you go to nursery school three mornings a week.

JEFFREY: Actually, these slides don't represent the most amazing part of our trip last year . . .

NICKY: I don't have anybody to play with.

JEFFREY: Our penetration into the bush.

SANDY: I didn't know you were allowed.

NICKY: I wish those children could come to my house.

JEFFREY: We penetrated the bush and saw things no human being has ever seen.

NICKY: Nobody plays with me.

SANDY: Oh, tell us everything!

JEFFREY: We encountered a civilization untouched by the Industrial Revolution. People living in the Stone Age.

The lights go dim and eerie.

SANDY: Ooooooooh, cave men.

JEFFREY: There are a bush people called the Whan See who are still arboreal.

Sandy gasps.

BILL: Jeeeez.

NICKY: I'm lonely.

BILL: Ssssssh!

JEFFREY: They live in trees and never come down to the ground.

MIA: What was so remarkable was that they were obviously Homo sapiens and not simian, yet they had this one extraordinary feature . . .

BILL: Christ, I hope you had your camera with you.

MIA: . . . a freakish biological throwback.

JEFFREY: Each and every one of them had a tail!

Sandy, Bill and Nicky gasp.

MIA: We couldn't believe our eyes the first time we saw them swinging through the trees. We'd been cutting our way through deep brush when we suddenly heard this chattering above us. It sounded like children giggling. We looked up. And there were these . . . people . . . swinging through the branches by their tails.

JEFFREY: Small boned with delicate features . . .

MIA: . . . and covered with this silvery down that glittered so brightly we had to shade our eyes.

Sandy, Bill and Nicky gasp.

BILL: *Did you get any pictures?*
MIA: And they had the most musical way of speaking . . . a kind of sighing almost.

Nicky picks up a cello and begins playing a Bach unaccompanied cello suite.

JEFFREY: We were afraid they'd run when they saw us, but they didn't. They just became very still and stared down at us.
MIA: I had no idea Nicky could play the cello so well.
SANDY: Oh, yes, Nicky's always been musical.
JEFFREY: Because they exuded such docility, I reached up my hand to one and said, "We're American anthropologists, we come in peace."
SANDY: What a perfect thing to say!
BILL: Beautiful . . . beautiful.
JEFFREY: They became very excited and all started talking at once.
BILL: At least you had a tape recorder on you.
MIA: I've never seen such eyes . . . a kind of creamy pink . . . like looking into a strawberry parfait.
SANDY: Weren't you scared?
JEFFREY: You see, we, without tails and wearing clothes, were just as strange to their eyes.
MIA: After Jeffrey spoke, I said a few words, and then our guide gave them some chewing gum. Then as a body, they furled and unfurled their long silvery tails and chanted, "Whan See." So we chanted it back.
JEFFREY AND MIA *(Chanting)*: Whan See, Whan See, Whan See . . .
JEFFREY: Then one of them motioned that we should join them. So we climbed a nearby tree and they gingerly approached us, touching our hair and skin.
SANDY: I would have died!
MIA: They were an exceedingly gentle people who had no words in their vocabulary for hate, anger or war.

JEFFREY: We spent an entire week with them.

MIA: It's amazing how fast you can adjust to living in a tree.

SANDY: I would have died . . .

JEFFREY: And not once in all that time did we ever see one of them drop down to the ground, even though they could stand erect, run, and even dance on their hind legs.

MIA: *You should have seen them dance!* They'd wrap their tails around a branch and start rocking back and forth, swaying higher and higher, then they'd suddenly let go and spin off through the trees like meteors . . .

JEFFREY: While the older members of the tribe banged on drums made of hollow tree stumps.

MIA: Our last day there they asked us to join them. The leader gripped me around the waist with his tail and started whirling me through the air. Everything was spinning and pulsating. There was this strong smell about him . . . cinnamon . . . cinnamon dust sprinkled through his fur . . . he spun me higher and higher and then suddenly . . . let go. We went flying through the air . . . his arms holding me close . . . oh . . . it was . . . just . . . everything rushing by . . . the sun on my face . . . the fragrance of cinnamon . . .

BILL: Jesus . . .

SANDY: Oh, Mia . . .

JEFFREY: Other tribes in the bush have repeatedly tried to capture the Whan See because of their great beauty and grace, but once a Whan See touches ground, he dies. Something happens to their center of gravity, their balance goes haywire.

SANDY *(Covering her ears)*: I can't listen . . .

BILL: Think of the shots you could have gotten with a Leica!

JEFFREY: In spite of their ignorance of science and technology, they displayed incredible artistic sophistication. They did these bark carvings with their teeth that were absolutely stunning!

MIA: It was a form of relaxation. They'd sit in the shade, tearing out the most intricate designs . . .

JEFFREY: Their virtuosity was astonishing. On the one hand, they did representational carvings depicting familiar bush objects, but then they also did these highly abstract designs that resembled some sort of ancient calligraphy.

MIA: And of course that constant gnawing on tree bark provided them with excellent dental hygiene.

SANDY: I've never heard anything like this.

JEFFREY: They also did exquisite lacework, tearing into large pawpaw leaves.

SANDY: You should write a book.

BILL: *Christ, I hope you got some pictures!*

MIA: The whole thing was like a dream . . . except . . .

JEFFREY: Except . . .

SANDY: Oh, no, they do something awful you haven't told us.

MIA: We didn't find out about it until our last night, otherwise we'd still be there.

JEFFREY: Neither of us wanted to leave. We'd have given up everything to stay with them.

MIA: Our careers, our fieldwork, our publications . . .

JEFFREY: Sometimes at night we'd watch them make love, their silvery bodies radiating a kind of shimmering electricity. And everybody would watch: children, parents, grandparents . . .

MIA: But that last evening we saw the flaw . . .

JEFFREY: . . . the stye . . .

MIA: . . . the moral defect.

SANDY: No!

BILL: *They eat their young!*

Sandy screams.

BILL: I knew it.

SANDY *(Covering her ears)*: Don't.

MIA: Our last evening there a young girl went into childbirth.

SANDY: Oh, no.

MIA: As usual, everyone gathered around to watch, since they had no awareness of modesty or privacy.

JEFFREY: No one doctor or midwife was in charge—the delivery was the responsibility of all the women of the tribe.

MIA: As the girl was in the final throes of labor, the older women reached out their hands to help her . . .

SANDY: I can't bear it, it will be awful!

MIA: Finally her moment came, the head appeared. She gave a shrill yelp of pain and joy . . .

Sandy gasps.

MIA: . . . and the baby was born . . .

SANDY: Oooooooh.

MIA: But the very instant it emerged, they lifted the tiny creature up and . . . and . . .

SANDY *(Hands flying to her heart)*: No!

MIA: It's too awful.

BILL: *One of the elders popped it into his mouth!*

Sandy screams.

MIA: They lifted the tiny creature up and reinserted it back into its mother's womb.

SANDY AND BILL: But that's impossible.

MIA *(Upset)*: And they did it again and again and again and again . . .

BILL: Son of a . . .

MIA: And the mother kept urging them on. As soon as the baby came out, she'd motion them to . . . stuff him back in. It was obviously some ritual, there was some minimal number of reinsertions a mother had to withstand.

SANDY: I don't believe it!

BILL: Now, that's one thing I'd have to see with my own eyes . . .

SANDY: It's barbaric . . . unnatural.

BILL: Did. You. Get. Any. Shots?

JEFFREY: Only the strongest survive.

BILL: If you got any pictures at all, you could sell them to one of the national magazines and make a bundle.

SANDY: But why? Why did she do it?

JEFFREY: You have to remember, these were a highly primitive people who took things literally. When a civilized woman has a baby, she too is possessive, only in more subtle ways. She's possessive of her birth experience and delights in retelling it. She's possessive of her baby and tries to keep him helpless for as long as possible. Well, these Stone Age women were just acting out those same impulses by forcing the baby back into its mother's womb. Through fetal insertion, you see, the primitive mother could experience her moment of motherhood again and again and again.

MIA: After the fourth insertion, her uterus went into profound shock. And how that baby squealed. It wasn't human after a while, but mangled . . . and drenched . . . like some rodent . . . some furry little . . . hamster.

SANDY: I'm going to be sick.

JEFFREY (Holding some slides up to the light): I've got to go through these and make sure I leave Nicky the right ones. Let's see . . . oh, yes, Caracas! What's this one of Nepal doing in here?

MIA: After a while they motioned me to join them and pulled me over to where she lay.

SANDY: I wish you'd stop this.

MIA: It was such a beautiful night, the air was so warm . . . I didn't understand what they wanted me to do at first, so I just stood there.

SANDY: I haven't been feeling well today. When I looked in the mirror this morning, I saw an old woman.

MIA: Then someone gripped my hand, guiding it towards the girl's birth canal. I felt something warm and moist. I looked down, I was holding the baby's head. Such a tiny head, about the size of a softball and covered with that same silvery fur, except it was wet and matted down. It was so slippery I was afraid I'd drop it, but then this hand closed over mine and brought the baby up against his mother's birth canal, which opened again, receiving him . . .

SANDY: I've been smelling the sea ever since I got up.

MIA: Her body convulsed, the baby came out again and again: five, six, seven times . . .

SANDY: My front teeth feel loose.

MIA: After a while I noticed that I was doing it myself, no one was guiding my hands, *I* was inserting the baby.

SANDY: I feel so tired all the time.

MIA: You know what it felt like? Stuffing a turkey. Stuffing a fifty-pound turkey with some little . . . hamster.

SANDY: Nicky . . . oh, my Nicky . . .

MIA: And there was this overpowering cinnamon smell. I started laughing.

SANDY: Nicky is four today. My son is four years old.

MIA: . . . and then everyone started laughing, with those light sighing voices. The women wrapped their arms around each other, threw back their heads and laughed.

SANDY: Oh, Mia! *You* should have a baby. It's so wonderful!

MIA: This great swell of musical sound rose up as the young mother stiffened and screamed, experiencing birth again and again.

SANDY: It couldn't have happened.

MIA: The baby died.

SANDY: Not even a Stone Age woman can withstand the abnormal.

MIA: The baby died.

SANDY: You're afraid.

MIA: It died in my hands.

SANDY: You're afraid to have a baby.

MIA: It just stopped moving and went all stiff.

SANDY: You're afraid something will be wrong.

MIA: The mother didn't realize.

SANDY: We're all afraid . . . but . . . it . . . isn't . . . like . . . that . . .

MIA: I was responsible and it died. *(She starts to cry)*

Nicky stops playing and puts his cello away.

SANDY: Of course there *are* sacrifices . . .

MIA: She'd fainted, and when she came to, she bared her breast to him and cupped his tiny head in her hand . . . but he didn't move . . .

SANDY: There are sacrifices.

BILL: There are sacrifices.

SANDY: For the first few years you'd have to stay home. You certainly wouldn't want to bring a newborn into the Sahara Desert or anything.

MIA: His tiny body fit into hers so perfectly.

SANDY: *There are sacrifices, but you gladly make them!*

BILL: You couldn't take an infant into some mud village with no sanitary or medical facilities.

MIA: She kept drawing his little head closer and closer.

SANDY: Your child's welfare always comes first.

BILL: It's difficult to imagine the sacrifices you have to make until you've actually had your own child.

MIA: Suddenly she sensed something was wrong. She looked up into the semicircle of women and searched their faces.

SANDY: You'd have to forget about your career for six or seven years, maybe even longer.

BILL: There'd be great resentment on your child's part if you left him to visit other children.

SANDY: Strangers, people you don't even know.

BILL: It's perfectly understandable.

SANDY: I wouldn't trade motherhood for anything in the world!

BILL: Sandy and Nicky are very close.

SANDY: Of course you could always adopt, but it just isn't the same as having your own.

MIA: She lifted the baby off her breast and held him tightly in her hands.

SANDY (*Leading Mia towards the floor*): It isn't like that.

BILL: Sandy and Nicky are very close.

MIA: Nothing happened, he didn't move. She breathed into his mouth. She slapped his face. She pulled at the down on his arms. She dug at his closed eyes with sticks, but . . . *nothing happened* . . .

SANDY (*Easing Mia onto her back*): It isn't like that . . .

MIA: *No life. Anywhere.* . . . She understood at last and screamed this scream.

SANDY: I knew it would happen tonight. I told Bill you'd change your mind, that you'd want your own.

MIA: Then in one awful moment, she hugged him close, stood up and jumped.

BILL *(Crouching next to Sandy and Mia)*: You can't really know about children until you've had your own.

MIA: Down they plunged and were lost in the night.

SANDY: It isn't like that. It just isn't like that. You'll see.

BILL: Sandy and Nicky are very close.

SANDY: Just relax and breathe. In . . . and out. . . . In and out. . . . In and out . . .

BILL *(Attending Mia as a doctor)*: Her pulse is racing.

SANDY: Breathe with the contraction, then exhale. In and out. . . . In and out . . .

MIA: . . . lost in the night.

BILL *(Breathing with Sandy)*: In . . . and out. . . . In . . . and out . . .

SANDY: Nicky, we need you too.

Nicky joins in with great concentration and flair. He takes blood pressure, administers shots, writes on charts. Their voices are disembodied, as if heard through a haze of painkillers.

JEFFREY *(Engrossed with his slides throughout)*: I'd completely forgotten about the Sook! They don't bury their dead, but prop them up against trees, like decorations. *(He looks through more)*

SANDY: We'll help you. We won't leave you.

BILL: In and out. . . . In and out. . . . In and out . . .

NICKY: Blood pressure: a hundred and fifty over two hundred and seventy-seven. Heart racing, irregular cardiovascular pattern.

SANDY: Don't stiffen up . . . relax and breathe . . . relax and breathe . . . *(Breathes with Bill)*

JEFFREY *(Holding up a slide)*: Lahore! Remember that afternoon we took a walk in the foothills!

SANDY: It's the most beautiful experience a woman can have. Breathe in . . . and out. . . . In and out . . .

Mia starts breathing in tempo with Sandy.

SANDY: Good girl. . . . That's right. . . . Hold it. . . . Let it out slowly . . .

MIA: Oh! Something's happening . . .

NICKY: Pulse: sixty over eighty. Blood pressure: two hundred and thirty over ninety-eight. She should be dilated about seven centimeters by now.

They all breathe faster.

MIA *(Screams in pain)*: *Oh!* . . . *Oh!* What's happening to me? I don't want this . . . please . . . I. . . . *Oh!*

JEFFREY: The Brazilian nomad has a life span of a hundred and twenty years, give or take a few.

MIA: In and. . . . *Oh!* . . . *Oh!* . . . *God! Help me!*

SANDY *(Holding her hand)*: You're doing just beautifully. The first is always the hardest.

BILL: The first is always the hardest.

NICKY: The first *is* always the hardest.

SANDY: . . . but the most rewarding.

BILL: Certainly the most rewarding.

NICKY: Absolutely the most rewarding . . .

MIA: *I . . . don't . . . want . . . this!*

SANDY: Concentrate on your breathing.

MIA: Can't you do something? *Can't you stop it? God!* . . . *Oh! Stop it!*

JEFFREY: Here's the skeleton of that goat we came across in Mexico.

BILL *(Struggling to hold her down)*: You'd better give me a hand. She's fighting.

SANDY *(Helping Bill)*: When you feel the contraction, push. Push. . . . Breathe. . . . Push. . . . Hold. . . . Push. . . . Breathe. . . . Push. . . . Hold. It's no good, she's fighting.

NICKY *(Sitting on her legs)*: She's going to pass out if she keeps up like this.

SANDY: She'll have to be put to sleep.

MIA *(Screaming)*: *Let me up. . . . Please stop this. . . . I want to get . . . Please. . . . Oh. . . . Oh!*

JEFFREY *(Looking at a slide)*: Lars Kronniger!

NICKY: *If you don't cooperate with us, you'll have to be put to sleep and miss everything.*

SANDY: That's right, you'll miss everything.

BILL: You don't want to miss everything, do you?

NICKY: Her pulse is four hundred and fifty over six and her blood pressure is six over four hundred and fifty. That can't be right!

SANDY: You've got to relax.

BILL: We'll have to put her to sleep.

SANDY: Push, hold, breathe. . . . Push, hold, breathe . . .

MIA: *I . . . don't . . . please. . . . I. . . . Oh! . . . You can't do this. . . . I. . . . Please. . . . Leave me alone. . . . Oh! You can't. . . . Oh . . . Ohhhh! (She passes out.)*

SANDY: They'd have such a beauti- ful baby.	BILL: It's no good when you fight it.	NICKY: What a shame. What a shame.

Silence.

SANDY: Well, I guess some women just . . . can't have children.

BILL: You can't pass a camel through the eye of a needle.

NICKY: One man's meat is another man's poison.

Silence.

SANDY: Well! What do you say we bring out Nicky's cake?!

The lighting returns to normal.

BILL: *Let's bring out Nicky's cake!*

NICKY *(Racing to the table)*: My cake, my cake, my cake . . .

BILL (*Prods Jeffrey away from his slides, escorting him to his seat*): We're bringing out the cake.

JEFFREY: It's funny about the slides of the Whan See. Not one of them came out. There must have been something in the down on their bodies that set off a toxic reaction to the film I was using.

BILL: Wait 'til you see this cake!

SANDY (*Lighting the candles on the table*): I just love candlelight.

NICKY: I get to make my wish now.

BILL: Sandy makes one hell of a birthday cake!

NICKY: I can't wait to make my wish.

SANDY: I wish Mia would get up and join us. It just isn't a party without her.

NICKY: I want Mia at the table.

SANDY: Why won't she get up?

BILL: I don't like this.

SANDY: Oh, Bill . . .

NICKY: What's wrong with Mia?

Silence. Jeffrey lifts Mia up from the floor, drags her to the table and sits her in a chair. Mia sits upright for several seconds and then slumps over.

JEFFREY: It happens all the time.

Silence.

SANDY: What have I done?

NICKY: Why won't Mia sit up?

BILL (*Lightly slapping Mia's face*): Come on, Mia . . . wake up . . .

SANDY: Oh, God.

JEFFREY: It won't do any good slapping her. When she's out, she's out.

SANDY: Oh, Bill . . .

BILL: Wake up, Mia!

NICKY: Is she dead?

Sandy screams.

BILL *(To Sandy)*: Maybe you should get some cold water.

SANDY *(Leaps up, gets cold water and sprinkles it on Mia's face)*: Mia? Mia?

BILL *(Lifts Mia up, holding her under the arms)*: Come on, let's walk her.

NICKY: She's dead. *She's dead!*

SANDY: She is not dead, she just passed out, that's all!

JEFFREY: It's pointless to do anything. She'll wake up when she's ready.

SANDY: She's not moving, Bill.

BILL: I know she's not moving. What do you think I am, blind?

SANDY: You don't have to yell!

NICKY: Mia's dead. Mia's dead!

SANDY: *Will you shut up, Nicky!*

BILL: Maybe I should lie her down on the floor again. *(He does)*

SANDY: Oh, Mia, I'm sorry.

NICKY: *You killed her!*

BILL: We did not kill her, she just fainted.

NICKY: *You killed her, I saw you kill her!*

JEFFREY: She'll pull out of it.

SANDY: I didn't mean to hurt you.

BILL: Isn't there any kind of medication that she carries with her?

JEFFREY *(Angry)*: I *told* you, there's *nothing* you can do. You never should have started all this in the first place!

SANDY *(To Bill)*: Prop her up again, she's so scary this way.

BILL *(Leaning Mia against a chair leg)*: There!

NICKY: You killed her.

BILL: *Stop it, Nicky, or it's back to your room!*

NICKY: How could you kill somebody on my birthday? Even *I* wasn't that bad.

JEFFREY: *Leave her alone!*

SANDY: I never should have said all that about having her own baby.

NICKY: I didn't . . . kill anybody!
BILL *(Raising his hand to him)*: Nickyyyyyy!
SANDY: I shouldn't have forced her.
BILL: You'd think she'd carry some kind of medication.

Mia slides down to the floor again with a thud. Sandy and Nicky scream.

BILL *(Peeling back Mia's eyelids)*: We must have some smelling salts or something . . .
JEFFREY: *I said, take your hands off her!*
NICKY *(Starts to cry)*: I'm scared.
BILL: Now what do we do?
JEFFREY: We finish the party so we can go home and forget the whole thing.
BILL: Yes! Let's bring out the cake!
NICKY: I don't want any cake.
BILL: Of course you want cake, it's your birthday. Sandy, get the cake.
SANDY: How can we eat birthday cake when she's . . .
BILL: *Get the cake!*
NICKY *(Cries)*: I don't like this party anymore.

Sandy exits to get the cake.

BILL *(Moving towards Mia)*: It would be nice if she could join us.
JEFFREY *(Out of his seat, pushing Bill aside)*: Don't touch her! You've done enough.

Jeffrey lifts Mia back to her seat, where she slumps over the table. Silence. Sandy enters carrying the cake, its candles blazing.

BILL: Isn't that some cake? Come on . . . let's sing!

Bill and Sandy sing "Happy Birthday" to Nicky. Sandy sets the cake down in front of Nicky.

BILL: Huhhhhh, is that *some cake*? Come on, Nick, let's hear your wish.

NICKY: I . . . can't.

BILL: Nicky can't make his fourth-birthday wish? I don't believe it!

SANDY: Oh, Nicky!

BILL: Come on, try.

Silence.

NICKY *(Concentrates, takes a deep breath)*: I wish . . . I wish I had a brother. *(Blows out the candles)*

BILL: Good old Nick, you never know what he's going to say.

SANDY: My Nicky . . .

BILL: That's quite a wish.

NICKY: I wish I had . . . three brothers!

SANDY *(Laughing)*: What about poor Mommy?

NICKY: I want three brothers to play with.

JEFFREY: All children need siblings.

BILL: Boy, that's all we need, three more kids.

JEFFREY: It would do Nicky good to have siblings.

NICKY: I'm lonely.

JEFFREY: The only child is more prone towards psychosis in later years . . .

NICKY *(Stamping his feet)*: I want three brothers for my birthday!

SANDY: He's overtired. We never should have let him come down from his room this afternoon.

BILL: Next time you'll stay in your room!

Mia slides to the floor with a thud. Grim silence.

NICKY: I want five brothers! No, I want eleven brothers . . . thirty-seven brothers . . . a hundred brothers . . . six hundred brothers! I want nine hundred brothers!

SANDY: Oh, Nicky . . .

NICKY: Nine hundred brothers!

SANDY: But don't we have fun together? We play Babies with the masks. We play Rabbit Says. Daddy makes videos of us.

NICKY *(Wailing)*: I want nine hundred brothers!

SANDY: I'd like to give birth to nine hundred more babies . . . but I can't.

NICKY: Why not?

SANDY: I've been trying.

BILL: We've been trying a long time.

SANDY: Ever since you were born.

NICKY: I'm lonely.

SANDY: There's nothing Mommy loves more than having babies, you know that, Nicky.

BILL: We've been to special doctors.

NICKY: I want someone to play with!

SANDY: No one can seem to find any medical reason why we can't conceive again, it's just one of those . . .

NICKY: I want to share my room with nine hundred brothers!

SANDY: The doctor said if you try too hard the mommy's eggs won't come down right.

BILL: Don't . . .

SANDY *(Teary)*: You see, every mommy has all these unborn eggs inside her and . . .

NICKY: I want a sister!

BILL *(His arm around Sandy)*: Honey . . .

SANDY: The timing has to be just right or else the egg won't turn into a baby.

NICKY: I want sisters!

BILL: He's too young to understand.

JEFFREY: The barren woman of the Gabon Tua tribe is considered a witch.

SANDY: It's such a wonderful feeling . . . life . . . fluttering . . . inside you . . .

NICKY: I want nine hundred brothers and nine hundred sisters!

JEFFREY: The barren Tot woman is taken out and drowned!

SANDY *(In tears)*: Sometimes I imagine I can still feel you . . . turning inside me . . .

NICKY: I'm lonely.

BILL: We haven't given up, Nicky. We're still trying!

JEFFREY: In Arabic cultures, the barren woman is . . .

BILL: *Will you shut up?!*

NICKY: I don't have anyone to play with.

SANDY: When I looked in the mirror this morning, I saw an old woman who could only conceive once.

JEFFREY *(Lifting Mia up under the arms)*: I don't know about you, but we've got a plane to catch tomorrow.

BILL: You can't leave, we haven't shown you our video of Nicky.

JEFFREY: We're flying to the tip of South America.

SANDY: My hair is falling out and I could only conceive once.

JEFFREY: A tribe of psychic toddlers is waiting for us.

Mia comes to, making little mewing sounds.

BILL *(Barring Jeffrey's way)*: Now just one minute, you said you'd see our video.

NICKY: I want to see the video, I want to see the video!

MIA *(Stretching)*: Uuuuuuuuuugh . . .

SANDY: Don't go.

BILL: We saw your slides. Fair is fair.

MIA *(Groggy)*: What happened?

NICKY: I want to see the video.

BILL: Show time!

NICKY: Show time!

MIA *(Rises, staggering around the room)*: Uuuuuuhhhhhhhh . . .

JEFFREY: We have two stopovers, one in Los Angeles and one in Rio.

NICKY: Movie time, movie time!

JEFFREY: We're talking thirty-eight hours in the air.

MIA: Ohhhhhhhhhh . . .

SANDY: Nicky was so looking forward to your watching it with us.

MIA: I feel as if I've been run over by a train!

JEFFREY *(Shaking Nicky's hand)*: Well, Nicky, it was a great party. We'll send you postcards. You can peel off the stamps for your collection.

BILL: You can't leave now, we're ready to roll.

NICKY *(Through an imaginary megaphone)*: *Show time!*

SANDY: *Show time!*

JEFFREY *(Kissing Sandy)*: Thanks for everything, Sandy. *(Shaking hands with Bill)* Keep the faith, Bill!

MIA *(Lurching around the room)*: Ohhhhh, I'm so dizzy.

NICKY *(Grabbing her hand)*: Don't go.

MIA: I have to.

NICKY: Stay.

MIA *(Cupping his face in her hands)*: Oh, Nicky . . .

NICKY: Please?

MIA: I can't.

NICKY: Pretty please?

A silence as Nicky and Mia stand gazing at each other.

NICKY *(Near tears)*: Pretty, pretty, pretty please?

MIA *(Putting her arms around him)*: Nicky, Nicky . . .

SANDY AND BILL *(Moved)*: Awwwww.

MIA: My brave boy.

NICKY: Don't go.

MIA: So big and strong.

JEFFREY *(Taking her arm)*: Mia . . .

SANDY *(Burying her head in Bill's chest)*: I'm going to cry.

JEFFREY: It's getting late.

NICKY *(Struggling to hold on to Mia)*: Don't go, don't go.

JEFFREY *(Pulling Mia out the door)*: Our plane leaves in six hours.

MIA: Goodbye . . . goodbye . . .

JEFFREY: We'll send stamps . . . lots of stamps!

And they're gone. Silence.

BILL: That son of a bitch.

SANDY: They left.

NICKY: They left.

BILL: We sat through his lousy slides, but do you think he had the courtesy to watch our video???! *(Imitating him)* "A tribe of psychic toddlers is waiting for us." *Jesus!*

Sandy sighs. Silence.

NICKY: *I want to see the video.*
SANDY *(Her hand flying to her mouth)*: Oh no!
BILL: Well, shit on him, we'll see it without them!
SANDY: My front tooth just fell out!
NICKY: I want to see my video!
SANDY *(Showing it to Bill)*: Look!
BILL: You'll see your video. Nick, don't worry.
SANDY: I'll have to call the dentist tomorrow. I can't walk around like this. *(Flashes a smile with a blacked-out front tooth)*
BILL *(Putting the videotape in the VCR and dimming the lights)*: All right, folks, is everybody ready for one hell of a show?
NICKY: Show time, show time!
SANDY *(Showing Nicky)*: Look at Mommy's tooth, Nicky. What do you think?

Bill sings a fanfare.

SANDY: It looks so . . . small . . . lying in my hand.
NICKY: Will the whole video be just me?
SANDY: The other one is loose too.

Images start up on the TV screen.

BILL: Hey, Nicky!
NICKY: Hey, Daddy!
BILL: Hey, Sandy!
NICKY: Hey, Mommy!
SANDY: Nicky on his fourth birthday . . . my Nicky . . .
BILL: *Four years old!*
NICKY *(Throwing his arms around Sandy and Bill)*: Look! Look! Look! Look!

They freeze in an endless embrace.

SANDY: Four years ago today, you made us the happiest family in the world!

The curtain slowly falls.

One Shoe Off

Characters

LEONARD, once an actor, 50s
DINAH, his wife, a costume designer, 40s
TATE, an editor, 40s
CLIO, his wife, an actress, 30s
PARKER, a director, 50s

One Shoe Off was originally produced by the Second Stage Theatre, New York City, Carole Rothman, Artistic Director and Suzanne Schwartz Davidson, Producing Director.

$\mathcal{A}$ct $\mathcal{O}$ne

SCENE 1

The ground floor of Leonard and Dinah's Greek-revival farmhouse in rural upstate New York. A slow-moving disintegration is at work, things are starting to fragment and sink into the ground. Rooms are drifting into each other leaving moldings, doorjambs and window frames stranded. The staircase, uppermost walls and ceiling vanish in midair. Grass, weeds and tangled shrubbery are encroaching indoors. Saplings and full-grown trees have taken root in the corners giving the place the look of a surreal ruin. It's early November around six in the evening. Leonard and Dinah are in their bedroom trying to decide what to wear. Dinah's in her slip and Leonard's in his underwear and a shirt. Both are barefoot. The bed and floor are littered with castoff outfits. The wind howls outside.

LEONARD *(Holding up an old sports jacket)*: What do you think?
DINAH *(Looking at herself)*: It's hopeless.

The wind rattles the windows.

LEONARD: Fucking wind.
DINAH: . . . hopeless!
LEONARD: Just listen to it.

They stand motionless, lost in their own worlds.

DINAH: *I don't know what to wear!*

LEONARD: One of these days it's going to blow the house down. That's all we need, to have the goddamned house flattened.

DINAH: Look at me!

LEONARD: You look great.

DINAH: But I'm still in my slip.

LEONARD *(Nuzzling her)*: Mmmm, you're so warm!

DINAH *(Resisting)*: Honey . . . ?

LEONARD: You're like a little furnace.

DINAH: They'll be here any minute.

LEONARD: So?

DINAH: I've got to get dressed.

LEONARD: Who says?

DINAH *(Heading into her closet)*: I hate this, I just hate it! *(She crashes around inside)*

LEONARD *(To himself)*: Forget it, she's out of here. *(He puts on the sports jacket)*

DINAH *(Emerges wearing a beribboned shepherdess dress)*: What do you think of this? *(She strikes shepherdess poses)*

LEONARD *(Engrossed in his jacket)*: I've always loved this jacket.

DINAH *(Starts herding imaginary reindeer)*: On Dasher, on Dancer, on Cupid and Vixen . . .

LEONARD *(Holding up two pairs of pants)*: Which pants do you think go better?

DINAH: On something and something and Donner and Blitzen?

LEONARD: The gray?

DINAH: Wait a minute, those are reindeer, not sheep! What's wrong with me?

LEONARD: Or the brown?

DINAH: Good old reindeer . . .

LEONARD *(Switching them back and forth)*: What do you think? Helloooo? You there . . .

DINAH: What *is* it about reindeer?

LEONARD: Bo Peep?

DINAH: They're so . . . what's the word . . . ? *(Pointing to the gray pants)* Nice pants!
LEONARD: Yeah . . . ?
DINAH: They look great, but then you look great in everything.
LEONARD: Hey, hey, what do you say? Forget the brown and go with the gray! *(He puts them on)*
DINAH: Isolated, that's it.
LEONARD: *Isolated . . . ?* What are you talking about?
DINAH: Reindeer. You never see them with other animals. . . . *(Pause) Oh honey, he's coming, he's finally coming!*
LEONARD: You're not planning to *wear* that, are you?
DINAH: After all this time.
LEONARD *(Disappearing into his closet)*: And now for a tie . . .
DINAH *(Catching a glimpse of herself in the mirror)*: God, look at me, I look like something out of the circus! *(She wriggles out of the dress)*
LEONARD: Which do you think would go best? The maroon one you gave me for my birthday or the one with the crickets?
DINAH: You're so lucky, you always look great. It's not fair.
LEONARD *(Emerging with several ties)*: Or how about the paisley one I spilled on?
DINAH: That's why I married you, come to think of it. You could wear a shower curtain and look good.
LEONARD *(Holding it up)*: Then there's this striped number Po-Po gave me last Christmas.
DINAH *(Putting her arms around him)*: Five hundred years later and you still take my breath away, it's uncanny!
LEONARD: Awww.
DINAH *(Suddenly pulling away)*: He's going to cancel. You know Parker, he always cancels at the last minute.
LEONARD: I still don't understand why you had to invite those creeps over. Claribel and Thaddeus, or whatever their names are . . .
DINAH: Clio and Tate.
LEONARD: The guy's an asshole.
DINAH *(Heading back into her closet)*: How can you say that?

LEONARD: Easy, he's an asshole.

DINAH: But you don't even know him.

LEONARD: So why did you invite him over?

DINAH *(Emerges wearing a fringed cowgirl outfit)*: What do you think of this? *(She strikes cowgirl poses)*

LEONARD: It's going to be a disaster.

DINAH: Remember how he used to pick you up and carry you around?

LEONARD: Who?

DINAH: Parker.

LEONARD: Parker . . . there's another one.

DINAH: I always loved that.

LEONARD: Dinah, what *is* that you're wearing?

DINAH *(Whipping it off)*: I know, I know, don't even say it.

LEONARD: Stay in your slip!

Dinah screams with frustration.

LEONARD: I mean what kind of name is that? Theo . . . ?

DINAH: Tate, *Tate*!

LEONARD: It's so pretentious, he sounds like an English butler. Can't you tell them not to come?

DINAH *(Picking up a variety of castoff outfits and holding them up to herself)*: No.

LEONARD: Why not?

DINAH: I just *can't*!

LEONARD: You know I don't like having people over.

DINAH: They're new here, they don't know a soul.

LEONARD: So?

DINAH: I'm trying to be nice.

LEONARD: What about being nice to me?

DINAH: What are you talking about. I *am* nice to you.

LEONARD: The evening's going to be a disaster.

DINAH: Don't worry, it will work out. Parker's cool, he can handle anything. He's a director.

The wind howls again.

LEONARD: You hear that . . . ?

DINAH: Remember *Cyrano* . . . ?

LEONARD: Fucking wind!

DINAH: I've never seen so many crazy people onstage at once.

LEONARD *(Sitting down on the bed)*: I can't take this anymore!

DINAH: What was the name of that lovesick actress who cried all the time?

LEONARD: Meg Benedict.

DINAH: *Eggs Benedict,* always in tears! Poor Parker, I've never seen anyone so besieged. Not that he seemed to mind. You know Parker and women.

LEONARD: Don't laugh, but I've always thought you had a thing for him.

DINAH: *Me?*

LEONARD: Your whole face lights up whenever you talk about him. I may be going out on a limb, but I've always suspected something once happened between you.

DINAH: Between Parker and *me?*

LEONARD: That's what I said. What is this, an echo chamber?

DINAH: Pull yourself together woman and *get dressed for God's sake!* *(She throws down the last of the castoff outfits and heads back into her closet)*

LEONARD: I'm right, aren't I? Something did happen between you.

DINAH: Between who?

LEONARD: Between Parker and you. Jesus . . .

DINAH *(Emerging in a green cocktail dress dripping with beads and sequins)*: My lizard dress! What do you think? *(She darts her tongue in and out)*

LEONARD: I think you need professional help.

DINAH: *I have nothing to wear!*

LEONARD: What do you mean, you have nothing to wear? Look at all this stuff.

DINAH *(Taking the dress off)*: But it's not mine.

LEONARD: You designed it.

DINAH: For shows, not myself. I can't dress myself, I don't know who I am. It's tragic.

LEONARD: I wouldn't go that far.

DINAH: You're so lucky, you look great in everything.

LEONARD: I'm not lucky, I have shitty luck.

DINAH: You do have shitty luck.

LEONARD: The worst.

DINAH: Don't say that! It's just asking for trouble.

LEONARD: You're right, I'm sorry.

DINAH: If you go around saying you have the worst luck, you'll *get* the worst luck. I mean, think of all the terrible things that could happen. Colon cancer, Parkinson's disease . . .

LEONARD: I'm sorry, I'm sorry . . .

DINAH: A sudden stroke, cholera . . .

LEONARD: *Cholera . . . ?*

DINAH: You ought to sink down to you knees and thank God for your blessings, I'm serious! *(Shutting her eyes and praying)* Thank you, God, for giving us so much. Good health, beautiful children . . .

LEONARD: We only have *one* child, Po-Po. God, I wish we saw her more often. *(Wailing)* Po-Po, Po-Po, I want Po-Po.

DINAH: Half an acre of land, exciting careers . . .

LEONARD: Speak for yourself, I haven't worked in eleven years.

DINAH: Food in the icebox, wonderful friends . . .

LEONARD: What friends? We don't have any friends.

DINAH: You're right, we *don't* have any friends, I forgot. *(Pause, she looks around the room)* Jeez, look at the place . . .

LEONARD: We used to have friends. The minute the going gets tough, they're out of here. Take Parker for example, the man hasn't called in five years.

DINAH: Six.

LEONARD: You'd think we had the plague or something. Arrogant son of a bitch.

DINAH: It's a mess! *(She pulls a rake out from under the bed and starts raking drifts of fallen leaves into piles)* Come on, give me a hand.

LEONARD: Who does he think he is, suddenly inviting himself over after six years of avoiding us? The prodigal son! *(He grabs another rake and joins her)*

DINAH *(Raking away)*: I can't keep up anymore.

LEONARD: It never occurs to him that *we* might have plans, that *we* have a life . . .

DINAH: Look at this, we're being buried alive!

LEONARD: You've been planning to invite our new neighbors over for months now, months. What are their names again?

DINAH: Clio and Tate.

LEONARD: They sound like a pair of goldfish. *(He stops raking and starts making fish faces)*

DINAH: They *do* sound like a pair of goldfish, how funny. You're right, the evening's going to be a disaster, we don't even know these people. There's no telling how they'll get along with Parker or what kind of shape he'll be in when he gets here. *How did we get into this? (Pause)* You know the trouble with us? We lack courage.

LEONARD: What are you talking about?

DINAH: Do you think we'll ever have to forage in the woods.

LEONARD: *Forage in the woods?*

DINAH: WE DON'T HAVE ANY MONEY!

LEONARD: Oh, that . . .

DINAH: Things are starting to get scary. *(She picks up a Chap Stick and starts reading the ingredients on the side)* Petrolatums, Padimate, Lanolin, Isopropyl, Myristate, Cetyl Alcohol . . .

The telephone suddenly rings. Both race to get it.

DINAH:	LEONARD:
It's probably Parker!	The telephone!
I'll get it, I'll get it!	I've got it, I've got it!

LEONARD *(Gets there first and grabs the receiver)*: Hello?

DINAH: Who is it?

LEONARD: Hey, Parker, son of a bitch!

DINAH: I knew it.

LEONARD: You're still coming, aren't you?

DINAH *(Trying to horn in)*: Hi, Parker . . .

LEONARD: Slow down, slow down, I can't understand a word you're saying.

DINAH: It's me, Dinah . . .

LEONARD *(Struggling with Dinah)*: Easy, honey, easy! *(To Parker)* Where are you?. . . . What . . . ? I can't hear you over the sirens . . .

DINAH *(Yelling into the phone)*: We can't wait to see you!

LEONARD: Dinah, please! *(Back to Parker)* I'm sorry, you were saying . . .

DINAH: Hey, I was in the middle of a . . .

LEONARD *(To Dinah)*: Can't you see I'm talking?

DINAH *(Imitating his rhythm)*: Nya, nya, nya, nya, nya nya!

LEONARD *(To Parker)*: Sorry, sorry, I'm back. . . . What are all those sirens in the background?. . . . Slow down, slow down, I can't hear you. *(Listening for awhile.)* No . . . ! Sweet Christ!

DINAH *(Going ashen)*: What happened?

LEONARD: Oh no.

DINAH: *Is he all right?*

LEONARD: Stop, stop!

DINAH: *WHAT HAPPENED?*

LEONARD: Right, I understand. . . . Hey, we'll do it another time. . . . Right, I will. . . . You too. *(He gazes at the receiver)*

DINAH: Is he O.K.?

LEONARD *(Hanging up)*: Goodbye.

DINAH: *What happened? (Pause)* Tell me! Honey please?

Leonard covers his face with his hands.

DINAH: I'm *dying*!

LEONARD *(Recovered)*: I don't believe a word of it. Not. One. Word.

DINAH *(Shaking him)*: A word of *what*?

LEONARD: What does he take me for? A half-wit?

Dinah mews with frustration.

LEONARD: The man's a congenital liar.

Dinah's mewing intensifies.

LEONARD: A mobile home breaking loose from its trailer and careening all over the highway . . . ? Three cars totaled and five people dead before it finally crashes into a truck in the opposite lane. . . . Get real!

DINAH: He's not coming?

LEONARD: He said it missed him by inches, *inches*!

DINAH *(In a tiny voice)*: He's not coming?

LEONARD: Wreckage and twisted bodies everywhere . . .

DINAH: I knew he'd cancel, I knew it.

LEONARD: He stayed with the victims until help came, but now he's so shaken up he has to go home.

DINAH: He does it every time.

LEONARD: I've heard excuses to get out of evenings, but *this* takes the cake.

There's a knocking at the door.

DINAH: It's Parker, he came after all!

LEONARD *(Full of affection)*: That son of a bitch, he almost got us that time.

DINAH *(Heads towards the door)*: I'll get it, I'll get it!

LEONARD: Coming, coming . . .

DINAH *(Suddenly skids to a stop)*: Oh no, I'm still in my slip! *(She rushes back into the bedroom)*

LEONARD *(Skidding to a stop)*: Whoops, I don't have any shoes on! *(Calling) Just a minute, just a minute! (He follows Dinah into the bedroom)*

The front door opens a crack, the wind howls.

CLIO *(Offstage)*: Hello . . . ?

TATE *(Offstage)*: Anybody home . . . ?

CLIO *(Creeping into view)*: Are you there?

LEONARD *(To Dinah from the bedroom)*: Flipper and Whosis!

DINAH: Oh no, I forgot all about them.

CLIO *(Walking into the living room)*: Yoo hoo, we're here!

SCENE 2

A split second later. Clio and Tate come creeping into the living room. She's breathtakingly beautiful, dressed in actressy clothes. He's rugged looking, wearing casual weekend gear. Because they've left the front door open, the wind howls louder than ever. Dinah and Leonard are still in their bedroom.

TATE *(Calling)*: Louis . . . ?

CLIO *(Correcting him in a whisper)*: Lawrence.

TATE *(Whispering back)*: Who *are* these people, anyway?

CLIO: Lawrence and Diana.

TATE: How did you get us into this?

CLIO: Or is it Dianne?

TATE: You know I don't like going out on weekends.

CLIO *(In a sing-song)*: Hellooooo . . . ? It's us . . .

TATE *(Pulling on her arm)*: Come on, let's get out of here while we've still got a chance.

CLIO *(Calling)*: Lawrence . . . ? Dianne . . . ? *(To Tate)* No, I was right the first time, it's Diana. Or is it Delilah? Oh God . . .

TATE *(Pulling harder)*: I want to go home, I don't like this.

CLIO: You don't like anything.

TATE: I don't like going out on weekends, you know that. It's my one chance to get caught up on my work.

CLIO: Work, work, work. . . . Can't you ever take a break?

TATE *(Turning to go)*: You can stay if you want, but I'm leaving.

CLIO *(Taking in the room)*: Holy mackerel . . .

LEONARD *(Suddenly comes rushing into the room)*: Come in, come in . . .

TATE *(Skids to a stop, under his breath)*: Shit!

CLIO: This is amazing!

LEONARD: We were just . . .

TATE: Too late!

LEONARD *(Pumps Tate's hand)*: Tad!

TATE: Louis!

CLIO *(Correcting Tate)*: Lawrence.

LEONARD *(Correcting Clio)*: Leonard.
CLIO *(Correcting Leonard)*: Tate!
LEONARD *(Pumps Clio's hand)*: Clara!
TATE *(Correctly Leonard)*: Clio!
LEONARD: Whoops!
TATE *(Softly to Clio)*: Thanks a lot, I'll remember this.
CLIO: I'm sure you will.
LEONARD: So glad you could make it. Come in, come in. Let
me take your coats.

They overwhelm him with coats, mufflers, hats and mittens.

LEONARD *(Dropping and retrieving them)*: Whoops . . . sorry,
I've got it, I've got it. . . . Good old wintertime . . . nothing like
it. . . . Whoops, there we go . . . *(He exits trailing their outerwear
after him)*
TATE: Well, this is quite some place . . .
CLIO: It's wild.
TATE: Great trees.
LEONARD: Please!
CLIO: Just wild!
TATE: How do you get them to grow indoors?
LEONARD *(Returning)*: You mean, how do you get them to stay
outdoors?!
CLIO: It's such a great idea.

Silence.

LEONARD *(Rubbing his hands together)*: So . . . ?

The wind howls with rising fury.

TATE: Oh sorry, I'm afraid we forgot to shut the ding. *(He
rushes over to it and slams it shut)*
CLIO *(Under her breath to Tate)*: The *door*!
TATE: That's what I said.
CLIO: No, you said, the ding . . .

TATE: The *ding*?

CLIO: Never mind. *(To Leonard)* What *is* it with the wind around here . . . ?

LEONARD: Don't get me started.

CLIO: I've never heard anything like it.

Tate opens the door again.

CLIO: Toto, what are you . . . ?

TATE *(Slams and opens it obsessively, finally slamming it for good)*: There we go, I just wanted to make sure it was shut tight.

CLIO: Well, we all have our little . . .

TATE: Why waste precious heat if you don't have to?

Silence. Then, Dinah pokes her head in the room. She's still in her slip.

CLIO: Dianne!

TATE: Delilah!

LEONARD *(In a whisper)*: You're still in your slip.

CLIO *(Whispering to Tate)*: What's her name?

TATE *(Whispering back)*: How should I know?

LEONARD *(Whispering to Clio)*: Dinah.

CLIO AND TATE: *Dinah!*

DINAH *(Trying to enter the room but stay hidden at the same time)*: Don't pay any attention to me . . .

TATE *(Starts singing)*:
Someone's in the kitchen with Dinah,
Someone's in the kitchen, I know ow ow ow . . .

CLIO AND TATE:
Someone's in the kitchen with Dinah
Strumming on the old banjo.
They're strumming fee, fie, fiddly-i-o . . .

DINAH: I just wanted to see what everyone was wearing. *(To Clio)*: Ohh, what a great dress.

CLIO: What, this old thing?

DINAH *(Dashing out of her room)*: I'll be right back.

CLIO: I've had it for years.
LEONARD *(To Dinah)*: Hey, where are you going?
TATE: Stay in your slip, you look great.
LEONARD: She does look great, doesn't she? *Dinah, come back!*

Silence.

CLIO: It's so nice to finally meet you.
TATE: So . . . how long have you lived here?
LEONARD *(Calling after Dinah)*: Honey . . . ?!
CLIO: We've been waving at each other for months now.
LEONARD: Don't mind her, she has a terrible time dressing herself.
CLIO: Don't we all.
TATE: Speak for yourself.
CLIO: I just did.
TATE: Well, well, aren't we in good form this evening.

Silence.

LEONARD *(Calling in a strangled voice)*: Dinah, please!
DINAH *(Enters, dressed in a spectacular toga)*: You called?

LEONARD:	CLIO:	TATE:
(Covers his eyes and moans)	Holy Moses!	*(Does a wolf whistle)*

DINAH: *Julius Caesar.* It's too much, isn't it?
CLIO: Look at you!
LEONARD: Honey, this is upstate New York, not the Roman senate.
CLIO: That's incredible . . .
DINAH *(Turns to go)*: I *knew* it was too much.
CLIO: Incredible!
LEONARD *(Grabbing her arm)*: Don't go!
CLIO: Look, Zoo-Zoo.
TATE: I see, I see.
CLIO: Where did you get that?
LEONARD: She made it.

DINAH *(Trying to pull away)*: I've got to change.

LEONARD: Don't leave me again!

TATE *(To Dinah)*: You made it?

DINAH *(Struggling with him)*: Leonard . . . ?

TATE: *Why?*

LEONARD: Because she's a costume designer.

CLIO: Of course! I knew your name was familiar!

TATE: Right, right.

CLIO *(Pressing Dinah's hands)*: You're wonderful!

DINAH: Why, thank you.

TATE: Clio's an actress.

DINAH: No kidding.

TATE: Onstage and off.

CLIO *(To Tate)*: What's *that* supposed to mean?

TATE: If the shoe fits, eat it.

A pause as everyone looks at Tate.

DINAH: Leonard's an actor too.

CLIO: No!

LEONARD: Was an actor.

DINAH *(To Leonard)*: Now, now . . .

CLIO: I didn't know that.

LEONARD: *Fucking bastards!*

CLIO *(To Tate)*: Did you know he was an actor?

TATE: I had no idea.

LEONARD: *Sons of bitches!*

DINAH: He was the best, the best.

CLIO: Wow, what were you in?

LEONARD: You wouldn't remember it was so long ago.

DINAH: *Cyrano, Richard the Second, Uncle Vanya* . . .

LEONARD: *Stupid assholes!*

DINAH *(Putting her hand on his arm)*: Honey . . . ?

LEONARD *(Whirling away from her)*: Don't touch me!

An awful silence.

DINAH: He also keeps bees.

CLIO AND TATE: Bees . . . ?

LEONARD *(World weary)*: Dinah . . . ?!

TATE: I love bees!

CLIO: I'm terrified of bees!

DINAH: Leonard's a naturalist.

LEONARD: I thought I was a fatalist.

TATE: My brother keeps bees.

DINAH: He has over five thousand.

CLIO *(Rushing towards the door)*: I'm getting out of here!

LEONARD: They're not in the house, I keep them out back.

DINAH: We'll have to give you some of our honey, it's the best in the area. Leonard markets it all over the state.

LEONARD: Bees are highly civilized, they put us to shame.

TATE: Bees are the best.

LEONARD: They *are* the best!

DINAH: Well, they certainly keep Leonard busy.

CLIO *(Hands over her ears)*: I don't want to hear.

LEONARD: I could watch them all day.

DINAH: And he often does.

LEONARD: Well, better beekeeping than acting, it's a lot safer.

TATE: I've never understood the impulse to perform.

DINAH: Me either.

TATE: It's always seemed slightly perverse. Oh well, one man's meat is another man's pistol.

CLIO: Poison.

TATE: That's what I said.

CLIO: No, you said "pistol."

The wind suddenly blows the front door open with a blast. The four freeze in terror. Clio rushes to Tate who puts his arms around her. Dinah stands rooted to the spot, hand over her heart. Leonard sways on his feet. Then just as suddenly the wind dies down. Clio gasps, Tate releases a long breath, Leonard and Dinah shudder.

CLIO: What was that?

TATE: Wee Willie Winkie.
DINAH AND LEONARD: Wee Willie Winkie?
LEONARD: God, there's a name I haven't heard in ages.
TATE:
Wee Willie Winkie runs through the town,
Upstairs and downstairs, in his nightgown;
Rapping at the window, crying through the lock,
"Are the children in their beds?
Now it's eight o'clock."

They all look at Tate. An uncomfortable silence.

DINAH *(To Leonard)*: So, how about shutting the door?
LEONARD: Right, right. *(He moves to the door)*
TATE *(Joins him)*: Here, let me give you a hand.

They hurl themselves against the door, slamming it shut.

TATE:
Diddle diddle dumpling, my son John
Went to bed with his trousers on . . .
LEONARD: So, what would everybody like to drink? We've got
beer, wine, vodka . . .
TATE:
One shoe off and one shoe on,
Diddle Diddle Dumpling, that's my John . . .
DINAH: Mineral water, ginger ale, orange juice . . .
TATE: Poised for the worst.

Silence, then to Tate.

LEONARD:	DINAH:
Well, what's *your* line	So, what do *you* do,
of work? *(To Dinah)*	Tate? *(To Leonard)* Oh,
Whoops, after you . . .	sorry, sorry . . .

Pause.

LEONARD:	DINAH:
Sorry, I was just wondering what *you* . . .	So, tell us what you . . . Whoops . . .

Pause.

CLIO: Tell them what you do, Dee-Dee!

TATE: Guess.

DINAH: Let's see . . .

LEONARD: Um . . . you write nursery rhymes.

TATE: Close, close . . .

DINAH: You illustrate nursery rhymes.

TATE: You're getting warmer . . .

LEONARD: You *are* a nursery rhyme.

TATE: Bingo!

CLIO: He's an editor.

TATE: You got it!
The girl in the lane, that couldn't speak plain,
Cried, "Gobble, gobble gobble . . . "

LEONARD: And where do you do this editing?

CLIO: Raven Books.

LEONARD *(Impressed)*: Raven Books? Wow, you don't mess around!

TATE:
The man on the hill that couldn't stand still,
Went "Hobble, hobble, hobble."

CLIO *(Putting on a funny voice)*: Hobble hobble, wiggle wobble!

DINAH: She sounds just like Enid Brill.

CLIO: Enid Brill?

DINAH: The woman who gallops around the countryside in her nightgown.

CLIO: *Her!*

LEONARD *(Imitating her)*: She talks through her nose.

CLIO: We see her every morning.

LEONARD: She's certifiable.

DINAH: She's my idol.

LEONARD: Her husband's a crop duster. You'll hear him in the spring. *(He mimes a low-flying plane)*

DINAH: They have eight children.

CLIO: She whips that horse as if her life depends on it.

DINAH: It does, she's fearless.

Leonard's crop dusting intensifies.

DINAH: Wait 'til you've lived here a few more years, you'll understand. Easy, Leonard, easy . . .

LEONARD *(Recovering)*: Sorry, sorry.

DINAH: You know what she dressed up as at Halloween? You'll never guess *(Pause)* A sieve.

CLIO AND TATE: A sieve?!

DINAH: She pulled the screen out of her back door, molded it over her head in a dome and stuck a broom handle between her legs. The year before she went as a rubber glove. Don't even ask.

LEONARD: Poor Enid Brill.

DINAH: There but for the grace of God go I. Well, I hope everybody likes carrots. *(She heads into the kitchen)*

LEONARD: So, what would you like to drink? We've got beer, wine, vodka, mineral water, ginger ale, orange juice . . .

TATE: Clee-Clee?

CLIO: I'll have some white wine if you've got it.

LEONARD: You're on. And you, Todd?

TATE: Vodka sounds good.

CLIO *(Correcting Leonard)*: Tate, *Tate!*

LEONARD *(Fixing the drinks)*: Coming right up.

DINAH *(Enters carrying a mountain of carrots with their tops still on)*: I'm back, miss me?

CLIO: Holy Moses . . .

TATE: Look at all those chariots!

CLIO: Where on earth did you . . . ?

DINAH: Help yourselves, I'm trying to get rid of them.

Clio and Tate each gingerly take one.

DINAH: They grow all over the house. In the kitchen, the den, the upstairs bathroom . . . Dig in, dig in!

Clio and Tate each take a tentative bite.

CLIO: Hey, these are delicious!
TATE: They're so sweet!

They crunch in tandem.

DINAH *(Offering the tray again)*: Take more, take more.

They do.

LEONARD: You should have tasted the acorn squash from our bedroom last year . . . *(Passing out the drinks)* Chloe? Ted?
CLIO *(Still engrossed with her carrot)*: Ohhhhh . . . these are fabulous! *(To Leonard)* Oh thanks . . .
TATE: Mmmmmm . . . ooooohhhh. . . . *(To Leonard)* Much obliged.

More happy crunching.

DINAH: Well, I hope you're in the mood for turkey.
TATE: Where did you grow that? Down in the basement with the cranboobies? *(He emits a hoot of laughter)*
DINAH: Whenever we have guests, I do Thanksgiving with all the trimmings. It's the only meal I'm really good at.
CLIO *(Reaching for the platter of carrots)*: More, more . . .
DINAH: Fall, winter, spring, summer, out comes the Butterball and Stove Top stuffing.
CLIO: Tate does Thanksgiving at our house.
LEONARD: Butterball and Stove Top all the way! We love processed food.

CLIO: He's a great cook. We're talking corn chowder, oyster stuffing, zucchini pilaf. . . . We can't move for weeks, weeks!

DINAH: An old friend was going to join us tonight, but he canceled at the last minute.

LEONARD: He came up with this incredible cock-and-bull story about a mobile home running amok on the highway . . .

TATE *(To Clio)*: Well, you do Christmas, fair is fair. That is, when you're home.

LEONARD: I mean, people aren't mowed down by houses.

DINAH: They're only buried by them.

CLIO *(To Tate)*: I've never missed a Christmas with you, never!

LEONARD: What does he take us for, total idiots?

CLIO *(To Tate)*: When have I ever missed a Christmas with you?

DINAH: You'd think we'd learn. He sets us up and lets us down . . .

TATE: Last year.

DINAH: Sets us up and lets us down.

CLIO: My plane was grounded, I was stuck in the airport.

DINAH: Six years and not a word.

TATE: For a week?

DINAH: The trick is not to let it get you, right?

CLIO *(To Tate)*: As if you'd notice, you're so wrapped up in your goddamned editing.

TATE: Now just one minute . . .

CLIO: Words, words, words . . . and they're not even your own.

TATE: Nice Click, very nice.

DINAH: Keep your hand on the tiller and your back to the wind! *(She picks up a nearby bottle of Worcestershire sauce and reads the list of ingredients on the side)* "Water, vinegar, molasses, sugar, anchovies, tamarinds, hydrolyzed soy protein, onions, salt, garlic, eschalots, spices and flavorings!" *(She slams the bottle back down)*

Silence. Clio and Tate resume munching on their carrots.

DINAH *(Gazing at Clio)*: You are so beautiful.

CLIO: Why, thank you.

DINAH: Your skin . . . *(Reaching out to touch it)* May I?

CLIO: Be my guest.

DINAH *(Caressing her cheek)*: Ohhhh . . . it's so soft. Feel, Leonard, feel . . .

Leonard hesitates.

CLIO: Go ahead, it's all right.

LEONARD *(Touching her cheek)*: Mmmmmm . . .

DINAH: Isn't it soft?

LEONARD: Not as soft as yours.

CLIO AND TATE: Awww . . .

LEONARD: I think you have the softest skin in the world.

CLIO AND TATE: Awwwww . . .

DINAH: It's like burlap.

TATE *(Reaching to touch Dinah's face)*: Burlap . . . ?!

DINAH *(Whirling away from him)*: Please?!

Silence. The phone suddenly rings. Everyone jumps.

LEONARD:	DINAH:
(Getting there first)	*(Racing to get it)*
I've got it, I've got it!	I'll get it, I'll get it!

LEONARD *(Picking up the receiver)*: Hello?

DINAH *(Trying to wedge in on him)*: Who is it, who is it?

LEONARD *(Into the phone)*: Parker!

DINAH: Parker . . . ?!

LEONARD: Um hmmm . . . um hmmm . . . yeah . . . yeah . . . Wow, that's great! You sure you remember the way? . . . O.K. twenty minutes. See ya. Bye. *(He hangs up. To Dinah)* He's coming.

CLIO: Who?

LEONARD AND DINAH: Parker Bliss.

CLIO: *Parker Bliss?*

TATE: The director?

DINAH: You know him?

CLIO *(To Leonard and Dinah)*: You know Parker Bliss?

LEONARD: He's one of our oldest friends.

TATE: What was the name of that terrifying movie he just made?

DINAH: We've known him forever.

TATE: You know, the one based on the true story about the couple that murdered their children.

LEONARD, DINAH AND CLIO: *Lullabye and Goodnight.*

TATE: *Lullabye and Goodnight!*

CLIO: It was incredible!

TATE: I couldn't sleep for weeks.

DINAH: Us either.

CLIO: The performances he got out of those children. They were just toddlers.

DINAH: Parker's always been great with kids.

LEONARD: Except his own.

CLIO: That scene where their mother dressed them in party clothes before she threw them in the freezer . . .

TATE *(Hands over his ears)*: Don't, don't.

CLIO: The look on that girl's face as her mother leaned down and folded the cuffs of her tiny white socks, just so . . .

TATE: She knew what was going to happen.

DINAH: She knew.

ALL: She knew.

TATE: I couldn't go near our freezer for months.

LEONARD: When Parker called this morning and said he was going to be in our neck of the woods, we insisted he drop by.

DINAH: We figured you wouldn't mind if he joined us.

CLIO: *Wouldn't mind?* I've always wanted to meet him.

DINAH: But then he called right before you came, claiming a mobile home had broken loose from its trailer on his way up.

LEONARD: It totaled three cars and killed five people before it finally crashed into a truck on the opposite lane.

CLIO AND TATE: Oh no!

DINAH: It missed him by inches.

LEONARD: Please! You can't trust a word the man says.

TATE *(With meaning)*:
Jack and Jill went up the hill
To fetch a pail of water.
Jack fell down and broke his crown,
And Jill came tumbling after.

CLIO: Don't mind him, he's editing a new annotated *Mother Goose*.

TATE *(With brio)*:
Then up Jack got and off did trot
As fast as he could caper.
To old Dame Dob, who patched his nob
With vinegar and brown paper.

CLIO: Ahh Tate, ever the brilliant mind.

DINAH: Well, the important thing is he's coming.

CLIO *(Leaning to Tate)*: Actually, you *do* have a brilliant mind, Tic-Tac.

TATE *(To Clio)*: Why thank you, Cliquot.

DINAH: He's coming, he's coming!

LEONARD *(To Dinah)*: I'll believe it when I see it.

DINAH *(Rises, freezing)*: God, look at me! I've got to change!

SCENE 3

An hour and a half later. Parker still hasn't shown up. Dinah's slumped in a chair wearing an old-fashioned cotillion dress. Leonard's pacing by the door. He keeps checking his watch. Clio and Tate are asleep on the sofa, a mound of carrot tops at their feet. Several moments pass.

LEONARD: Nine forty-one . . .

DINAH: Honey, please.

LEONARD *(Continuing to pace)*: Nine forty-two.

DINAH: You're driving me crazy!

LEONARD: An hour and forty minutes late!

DINAH: Not so loud, you'll wake them up.

LEONARD: *Manipulative son of a bitch!*

Clio groans and stirs.

DINAH: Gently, gently . . .

LEONARD *(In a strangled whisper)*: Who the hell does he think
he is?

DINAH: He probably got lost.

LEONARD: Tell me another one.

DINAH: He'll show up.

LEONARD *(Resumes pacing, looks at his watch)*: Nine forty-three!

DINAH *(Suddenly rises)*: *I can't take this anymore!*

Clio and Tate stir in their sleep.

LEONARD *(As if seeing her for the first time)*: Honey, what *is* that
you're wearing?

DINAH: Amanda Wingfield, the dinner party scene with the
Gentleman Caller.

LEONARD: Let me out of here!

DINAH *(Striking flirty poses)*: What do you think?

LEONARD: This is a madhouse.

DINAH: Be honest, I can take it.

LEONARD: I want to go home.

DINAH: You *are* home. *(Dashing out the room)* Hang on, I'll be
right back.

LEONARD: Where are you going?

DINAH: To change.

LEONARD: Not again!

DINAH: I'll just be a sec.

LEONARD: This is getting perverse.

DINAH *(From the bedroom)*: What did you say?

LEONARD: I SAID, THIS IS GETTING PERVERSE!

Tate and Clio wake like a shot.

TATE: Perverse? Who . . . ? Where . . . ?

CLIO: Did somebody say "perverse"?

LEONARD *(Waving to them)*: Welcome back to the land of the living.

CLIO *(Groggy)*: Ohh, where am I?

LEONARD: Still waiting for Parker.

There's a loud crash from the bedroom.

CLIO *(Jumping)*: What was that?

LEONARD: Easy, Dinah, easy . . .

TATE *(Looking at his watch)*: Good God, look at the time.

A series of crashes from the bedroom.

DINAH *(From the bedroom)*: It's all right, it's all right, not to worry . . .

LEONARD: Poor Dinah, getting dressed always throws her into a tailspin. It's one of life's ironies—the costume designer who doesn't know what to wear.

Dinah enters swathed in a jingling harem outfit with pointy gold shoes. Leonard covers his eyes and groans.

DINAH *(Brandishing a scarf)*: *Peer Gynt.* What do you think?

CLIO: Heaven, *heaven!*

TATE: What happened to Amanda Wingfield?

CLIO *(Grabbing the scarf)*: I want it!

TATE: I've always been a sucker for faded Southern belles.

LEONARD *(Peeking at Dinah between his fingers)*: Sweetheart . . . ?

DINAH: God, look at it in here! *(She grabs a nearby rake and starts raking the carrot tops)*

LEONARD: We need to have a little talk.

Dinah keeps raking as Clio launches into a sexy belly dance.

TATE: Clee-Clee, this isn't the Casbah!

Clio dances with rising abandon. Everyone watches, enthralled.
Suddenly there's a loud knock on the door. They all jump.

DINAH:	LEONARD:	CLIO:	TATE:
He's here,	Well, what	It's him!	At last!
he's here!	do you		
	know?		

DINAH:		LEONARD:	
(Getting there first): I'll get		(Two steps behind): I've	
it, I'll get it!		got it, I've got it!	

Parker stomps in, shaking a blizzard of snow off his head and
shoulders. He wears work shoes and a parka with an enormous fur-
lined hood. He scoops Dinah up in his arms and whirls her around
in circles.

PARKER: Dinah, Dinah . . .

DINAH *(Clinging to him)*: Oh Parker . . .

PARKER: Sorry I'm so late, I got lost.

CLIO *(Gazing at him in rapture)*: Parker Bliss . . .

TATE: It's snowing?

LEONARD: HEY, PARKER . . . !

TATE: When did it start snowing?

CLIO: I'm going to die.

PARKER *(Showering Dinah's face with kisses)*: Threads,
Threads . . . !

LEONARD *(Trying to horn in)*: YOU OLD SON OF A BITCH!

DINAH: I've missed you so!

PARKER *(Thrusts Dinah out at arms' length)*: Hey, sweet thing,
let me get a good look at you!

DINAH *(Reaching for him)*: Come back, come back!

PARKER *(Pointing at her dress)*: *Peer Gynt,* the Olympic Theater!

DINAH: You got it!

LEONARD: "Anitra, oh thou true daughter of Eve, how can I
refuse you? I am but a man."

PARKER *(Bursts out laughing, scooping Dinah back into his arms)*:
You're too much, too much!

LEONARD (*To Clio*): Like I said, we've done a lot of shows together—Washington, Philadelphia, New York . . .

TATE (*Goes to the door and gazes out*): Boy, look at it come down.

CLIO (*Shivering*): Oooh, shut the door, Robert, that wind is wicked!

TATE: Robert? Who's Robert?

Parker squeezes Dinah tighter and roars.

CLIO (*All innocence*): Robert?

TATE: You just said, "Shut the door, Robert, that wind is wicked."

CLIO: I did?

TATE: As clear as a bell.

CLIO: You've lost your mind.

TATE: Not my mind, just my bearings. (*He plunges out the door*)

CLIO (*Starts to follow him*): Toto, where are you going? It's freezing out there!

DINAH (*To Parker*): Hold me, hold me.

PARKER (*Squeezing her tight*): It's been so long.

DINAH (*Barely audible*): My dearest, my darling . . .

CLIO (*Re-entering the room*): Don't mind him.

LEONARD (*Dancing around them*): When do I get my turn? I want my turn!

PARKER (*Lifting Dinah off her feet*): God, I love this woman!

LEONARD (*Trying to pull Parker and Dinah apart*): No fair, no fair! What about me?

PARKER (*Finally catches Leonard's eye and starts laughing*): Hey Handsome, how are the bees?

LEONARD: *Busy!*

PARKER: Come on, get over here.

They roar and pummel each other.

PARKER (*Grabs Leonard in a bear hug and kisses him square on the lips*): MAA! (*Holding him at arms' length, laughing*) Look at you, you crazy son of a bitch!

LEONARD: I *am* a crazy son of a bitch, aren't I?
PARKER *(Imitating him)*: "I *am* a crazy son of a bitch, aren't I?"
Jesus Christ, you never change.

They start air boxing.

DINAH *(To Clio)*: Men . . .
CLIO: Please!
DINAH: They're such little boys.
CLIO: You should see Tate when he gets together with his friend
Walter. Forget it!
DINAH: Where *is* Tate, by the way?
CLIO: *Who knows!*

*There's a sudden banging on the front door. Leonard and Parker
stop air boxing.*

DINAH: Goodness, who can that be?
CLIO: Beats me.
LEONARD *(Heading towards the door)*: Well, there's one way to
find out.
DINAH: Careful now, there are all kinds of maniacs out there.

The knocking gets louder. No one moves.

PARKER: I'll get it. Let me. *(He opens the door)*

*Tate stands shivering on the threshold, a light mantle of snow
dusting his head and shoulders.*

PARKER: Yes, may I help you?
TATE: Ohhhhh, it's freezing out there!
LEONARD: Todd!
CLIO: Zum-Zum!
DINAH: Tate!
CLIO: There you are!
DINAH: Where have you been?

TATE: I just stepped out for a fresh of breath air.

LEONARD: Come in, come in.

TATE *(Entering, stomping snow off his feet)*: Oooohhhh!

LEONARD *(Introducing him to Parker)*: Todd, Parker. Parker, Todd . . .

TATE *(Extending his hand)*: Parker!

PARKER *(Shaking it)*: Todd!

CLIO *(Touching Parker's arm)*: Tate!

PARKER *(Finally seeing her)*: *You!*

CLIO *(Staring back)*: Parker Bliss . . .

PARKER: Clio Hands . . .

DINAH: You know each other?

PARKER: *I don't believe it!*

CLIO: I'm speechless.

PARKER: I adore you!

Silence as they gape at each other.

DINAH: When did you meet?

PARKER: We've never met. *(Takes her hand and kisses it)*

DINAH: Oh.

Leonard ushers Parker into the living room.

LEONARD: Well, come on in and stay awhile. Take off your parka, Parker. *(He laughs at his cleverness)*

PARKER *(Rooted to the spot)*: Clio Hands . . .

TATE *(Strides over to Clio, pulling her close)*: Hi, Coco.

PARKER: I must be dreaming.

CLIO: Hi, Totes.

TATE: How're you doing?

CLIO: Fine, fine . . .

PARKER *(To Leonard and Dinah)*: Didn't you see *Tiger Bright*?

LEONARD AND DINAH: *Tiger Bright*?

TATE *(Under his breath)*: Here we go . . .

PARKER: The movie.

LEONARD *(To Clio)*: You were in *Tiger Bright*?

PARKER: She was a vision . . .

LEONARD: I didn't know that.

PARKER: A vision.

DINAH: Gosh.

LEONARD: So, you're a movie star?

CLIO: Hardly, it was my first film.

PARKER: That scene where you danced with the dwarf. . . . *(He groans)* She smiled this smile . . . her lips started to tremble, or should I say melt. . . . No one in the theater could breathe. *(Gesturing, he brushes Clio's breast)* It was as if she'd handed us her soul.

TATE *(Quickly pulling her away from Parker)*: That's my Clicker.

Clio walks away from them both.

DINAH: Well . . .

Silence.

DINAH: And how's Patsy these days?

LEONARD: Yeah, how *is* Patsy?

CLIO: Patsy?

DINAH: His wife.

CLIO: Oh.

PARKER: Fine.

DINAH: I love Patsy.

PARKER: Everyone loves Patsy.

DINAH: Well, she's a great woman.

PARKER: Tell me about it.

Silence.

LEONARD: Come on, take off your coat and stay awhile.

Parker takes it off, revealing a large dried bloodstain on his shirt. Everyone screams.

LEONARD:	DINAH:	CLIO:	TATE:
Jesus	Parker . . . ?!	Blood!	Are you
Christ!			all right?!

LEONARD: You were telling the truth!

DINAH: A mobile home *did* run wild!

TATE: Holy shit!

CLIO *(Covers her eyes and sways)*: Oh God!

Parker collapses in a chair, burying his face in his hands.

DINAH *(Rushing over to him)*: Oh Parker . . .

LEONARD: Son of a bitch . . .

DINAH: Baby, baby . . .

CLIO *(Sinking into the sofa)*: I'm going to faint.

LEONARD: I thought you made it up.

DINAH *(To Parker)*: Speak to me.

LEONARD: I'm stunned.

Clio faints.

TATE *(Rushing over to Clio)*: Darling . . .

DINAH *(To Parker)*: Say something!

LEONARD: He was telling the truth all along.

TATE: Can you hear me?

LEONARD: You could knock me over with a feather.

Clio comes to and groans.

TATE *(Grabbing her hands)*: My beauty, my sweet . . .

CLIO: Whoooooo . . .

TATE: What happened?

DINAH *(Unbuttoning Parker's shirt)*: Here, let's get you out of this.

Dinah eases it off him. The blood has seeped through to his undershirt.

DINAH:	CLIO:	LEONARD:	TATE:
Uughhh!	More blood!	Jesus Christ!	Oh no . . . !

Clio passes out again as Dinah helps Parker off with his undershirt. Traces of blood linger on his chest. More horrified gasps.

DINAH: Baby, baby, does it hurt?
PARKER: It's not my blood.

Dinah recoils from him with a groan.

LEONARD: Whose *is* it?
TATE *(To Clio)*: Speak to me!
PARKER: It's from the ten-year-old boy who died in my arms.
LEONARD: Oh God!
CLIO *(Coming to)*: Where am I?
TATE *(To Clio)*: Right here, safe and sound with me.
PARKER: His car was sliced in half by the thing.
DINAH: Awful, awful . . .
PARKER: It was the strangest sight . . . seeing this *house* plowing down the highway.
LEONARD: He's cold, Dine, get him something to put on.
DINAH: Right, right . . . *(She exits)*
PARKER: It was a split-level ranch with redwood siding.
TATE: He's in shock.
PARKER: I saw a woman through the window. She was doing the dishes in the kitchen sink, washing this huge enamel pot. You know, one of those black and white speckled things you cook corn or lobsters in. . . . She was scrubbing it with this yellow brush. . . . I've never seen such a color. It was that neon yellow students underline textbooks with—only brighter. But how could that be? People don't live in those giant mobile homes when they're being transported, and they certainly don't do the dishes while they're moving. Yet I saw her as clear as day. . . . There was no sign of her after the crash, though. . . . Strange. . . . It's a miracle more people weren't killed when you

stop to think about it. A fifty-ton split-level ranch ricocheting across a four-lane highway. . . . It's a wonder any of us escaped.

DINAH (*Returning with an assortment of kingly robes and doublets*): Here, I brought you some things from my collection.

PARKER: Eeny, meeny, miney, moe.

LEONARD: Dinah, this isn't a play.

Silence.

CLIO (*To Dinah*): Didn't you do the costumes for that wonderful *Hedda Gabler* we saw at the New York City Festival a few years ago?

TATE: I remember that, lots of starched linen and high button shoes.

DINAH: You saw it?

CLIO: We see everything at the Festival.

LEONARD: She also works at Baltimore Rep, the Boston Theatre Company, Altered Stages . . .

CLIO: You're a busy woman.

DINAH: A frantic woman!

PARKER: Ohhh, I'm freezing. (*Reaching for a robe*) Let me have one of those, would you?

DINAH (*Handing him one*): God, what *was* that from?

CLIO: Ohh, it looks great.

PARKER: Yeah?

DINAH: *Pericles? Coriolanus?* (*Adjusting the shoulders*) It fits perfectly.

CLIO: Well, the woman's a brilliant designer.

PARKER: Hear, hear.

DINAH: Uuugh!

LEONARD: *Richard the Second.*

DINAH: *Richard the Second!*

CLIO: I love that play.

PARKER: It's the best, the best.

LEONARD:
For God's sake let us sit upon the ground,
And tell sad stories of the death of kings . . .

DINAH: Talk about ancient history . . .

PARKER: Sold out every night.

LEONARD:
How some have been deposed, some slain in war,
Some haunted by the ghosts they have deposed,
Some poisoned by their wives, some sleeping killed . . .

DINAH: You should have seen Leonard.

LEONARD:
All murdered . . .

DINAH: He was so handsome, he looked like a god.

CLIO: He still does.

DINAH *(To Leonard)*: You hear that?

CLIO: You've got great bones.

PARKER: Why do you think I call you Handsome, Handsome?

DINAH: Ahhh, the lure of beauty.

TATE: The lure of beauty . . .

DINAH: It's a killer, a killer.

LEONARD *(Grabbing a robe and putting it on)*:
For within the hollow crown
That rounds the mortal temples of a king
Keeps Death his court; and there the antic sits,
Scoffing his state and grinning at his pomp . . .

PARKER *(Unsheathes an imaginary sword and starts doing* Henry V *)*:
Once more unto the breach, dear friends, once more,
Or close the wall up with our English dead . . .

LEONARD: *Henry the Fifth!*

CLIO: Go for it!

LEONARD *(Entering into the spirit)*:
But when the blast of war blows in our ears,
Then imitate the action of the tiger.
Stiffen the sinews, conjure up the blood . . . *(He pauses, unsure of the words)*

DINAH: Disguise . . .

LEONARD:
Disguise fair nature with hard-favored rage . . .

PARKER:
Cry havoc and let slip the dogs of war!

Parker links arms with Leonard and starts marching around the room with him.

PARKER: Hut, two, three, four; hut, two, three four . . .
DINAH: And they're off—The March of the Kings!
PARKER AND LEONARD: Hut, two, three, four; hut, two, three four . . .

Parker toots an imaginary trumpet and Leonard mimes playing a xylophone.

DINAH: Don't mind them, this is something they do.
CLIO: Hey, wait for me! *(She dashes in front of them and mimes being a baton-twirling drum majorette)*

They march around the room with rising gusto.

PARKER: About . . . face!

The band switches direction and function. Parker plays a trombone, Clio bangs a drum and Leonard becomes the baton-twirling drum majorette.

PARKER: Fall out! *(Sweeping Clio into his arms)* Well, you're quite an accomplished little musician.

Leonard continues to march, tossing an imaginary baton.

CLIO: I played trumpet in my high school band.

Parker keeps Clio in his embrace; they lock gazes.

TATE *(Taking Clio's arm)*: Clio's a woman of many talons.
PARKER: So I see.
DINAH *(Linking arms with Parker)*: Still the same old Parker.
TATE: She acts, she marches, she plays musical elephants . . .
CLIO: Come on Toto, let up.

Dinah and Tate separate Parker and Clio. Leonard keeps marching around the room tossing his baton.

DINAH: Leonard . . . ?

PARKER: Go Handsome!

DINAH: Don't encourage him.

LEONARD: Hut, two, three, four; hut, two, three, four . . .

PARKER *(To Dinah)*: So, you're here year-round now?

DINAH: This is it. Just me, Leonard and the bees.

PARKER *(To Clio and Tate)*: They used to have the most magnificent apartment on Central Park West.

CLIO: No kidding.

DINAH: Leonard inherited it from an aunt.

PARKER: Ceilings up to here, and forget the view.

TATE: We have a place there too.

DINAH: But then things got tough and we had to sell.

LEONARD *(Whirling in the opposite direction)*: About face!

TATE: In the Beresford.

DINAH: I don't want to hear.

CLIO: What a coincidence!

TATE: The top two floors.

DINAH *(Hands over her ears)*: Don't!

LEONARD: Double time! *(He marches and tosses in double time)*

DINAH: Oh well, easy come, easy go.

CLIO: We've just bought a summer place here.

PARKER: Ahhh—

TATE: We're renovating the Van Alstyne mansion next door. Fourteen rooms and six fireplaces.

CLIO: It's a nightmare.

DINAH: Leonard, you're making me dizzy!

Leonard comes to a stop.

PARKER: Renovations always are. *(Pause)* So, what do you do, Todd?

CLIO *(Correcting him)*: Tate.

TATE: I'm a scream writer.
DINAH: Wait, I thought you said . . .
TATE: I write screams.
CLIO: Don't listen to him, he's pulling your leg.

Tate suddenly screams very loud. Everyone freezes.

CLIO: He's an editor.
PARKER: Well, well . . .
CLIO: Editor-in-chief, as a matter of fact.

Tate screams again.

CLIO: He's head of Raven Books.
PARKER: Whoa, that's one of the classiest publishing houses in the country!
TATE: So I'm told.
LEONARD: Well . . .

Silence.

LEONARD *(To Dinah)*: Sweetheart, haven't you forgotten something?
DINAH: Who, me?
LEONARD: It starts with "D."
DINAH: Let me think. Um, drinks, hors d'oeuvres . . .
LEONARD *(In a whisper)*: Dinner.
DINAH *(In a panicked little voice)*: Dinner?
LEONARD: It's almost eleven o'clock.
DINAH: Oh my God . . .
PARKER: Thanksgiving with all the trimmings?
LEONARD: Thanksgiving with all the trimmings!
DINAH: *Dinner!*
TATE: You need any help?
PARKER *(To Clio and Tate)*: It's the only meal she ever makes. Birthdays, Easter, Fourth of July, out comes the Butterball.

CLIO: Tate does Thanksgiving at our house.

DINAH: DINNER . . . ! *(She hikes up her skirts and dashes into the kitchen. She starts hurling pots and pans every which way)* Start the beans, fix the cranberry sauce, finish the sweet potatoes . . .

CLIO: He's a great cook.

PARKER: Lucky you. *(Drifting over to her again)* And lucky Tate.

CLIO *(Gazing into Parker's eyes)*: Why, thank you.

TATE: Lucky Tate, that's me all right. Yes siree, Bob, I've got it all.
Old King Cole
Was a merry old soul
And a merry old soul was he,
He called for his pipe
And he called for his bowl,
And he called for his fiddlers three . . .

There's a series of loud crashes from the kitchen.

DINAH: Whoops . . . easy does it, easy does it.

LEONARD *(Yelling to Dinah)*: ARE YOU O.K. IN THERE?

DINAH: FINE, FINE, NOT TO WORRY. . . . Open the cranberry juice, dump it into a bowl, add a little orange juice, cut up some celery . . .

TATE:
Every fiddler, he had a fiddle,
And a very fine fiddle had he . . .

CLIO: Don't mind him, it's stress.

PARKER: Ah, stress.

LEONARD: Good old stress.

CLIO: He works too hard.

Silence.

DINAH *(Rushing back into the room, wearing an apron)*: Talk, talk, everything's under control. It will just be a couple of minutes. *(She dashes back to the kitchen)*

Silence.

TATE: I've always liked Old King Cole, he knew how to enjoy life. He had his pipe, his bowl, his fiddlers three. . . . I've often wondered if he was married. If there was an old *Queen* Cole in the picture. What do you think, Clee?

CLIO: I have no idea.

TATE: Maybe it was the *absence* of a wife that made him so merry. He didn't have to worry what she was up to all the time. What do you think?

CLIO *(Getting upset)*: I said, I don't know.

TATE: I say he was unencumbered.

CLIO: Totey, please . . .

Silence.

DINAH *(Re-enters the room)*: Talk, *talk!* *(She waits)*

The silence deepens.

LEONARD *(To Parker)*: So . . .

Dinah rushes back to the kitchen.

LEONARD *(To Parker)*: . . . how come you never call?

PARKER: Never call?

LEONARD: It's been six years and not a word, a murmur, a sneeze. I thought we were friends.

PARKER: We are friends.

DINAH *(From the kitchen)*: OH NO, I DON'T BELIEVE IT!

LEONARD: I haven't worked since *Cyrano.* It's been eleven years, *eleven years!* You're a big director now . . . movies, TV specials every other week. . . . Why won't you hire me?

PARKER: I was almost killed a couple of hours ago.

LEONARD: I was your favorite actor!

PARKER: A ten-year-old boy died in my arms.

LEONARD: I need a job.

PARKER: You know what he kept saying?

LEONARD: This is a tough business, I'm not getting any younger.

PARKER: "I've got a stitch in my side."

LEONARD: I need all the help I can get.

PARKER: *"I've got a stitch in my side!"*

LEONARD: I'm going crazy.

DINAH *(Staggers in, carrying an enormous raw turkey)*: LOOK, I FORGOT TO TURN THE OVEN ON!

TATE: Oh no!

DINAH: Snow-white and cold as ice.

LEONARD: Dinah supports us now.

PARKER: His legs were severed at the knee.

LEONARD *(Indicating the turkey)*: There I am . . .

PARKER: They were lying on the hood of his car.

LEONARD: Dead meat!

PARKER: It could have been me, so kick up your heels while they're still attached.

DINAH: What am I going to do?

TATE *(Taking the turkey from her)*: Not to worry, I'll just filet it into cutlets, dust them with a little rosemary and olive oil and stick them under the broiler. They'll be ready in no time. *(He exits to the kitchen)*

DINAH *(Near tears)*: I'm so ashamed.

PARKER: Drain the cup and dance the dance.

DINAH: Everything was going to be perfect.

LEONARD: So, it's dancing you want. I'm versatile, what are you looking for? A little soft shoe? *(Doing as he says)* A little tap?

DINAH: My one foolproof meal . . .

CLIO *(Heading towards the kitchen)*: Well, I think I'll go see what Tate's up to.

Leonard taps in front of her, deliberately blocking her way.

CLIO: Excuse me, I was just . . . *(Trying to get past him)* Sorry, sorry . . .

LEONARD: I may not be as young as I once was, but I still have technique.

DINAH: This is getting scary.

Clio finally manages to escape.

LEONARD: No, wait! I know, you're looking for something a little more south of the border. You're just a stone's throw away from Mexico these days. Why didn't you say something? *(He starts doing flamenco steps)*

DINAH: Everything's out of control.

PARKER: Easy, Handsome, easy . . .

LEONARD: I'm intuitive, but I'm not a mind reader. *(He dances with rising gusto, adding yelps and handclapping)*

DINAH: Parker's homecoming, and look at us. I'm a wreck, you're dancing the flamenco, and our guests are making dinner!

And the curtain quickly falls.

$\mathcal{A}$ct $\mathcal{T}$wo

SCENE 1

An hour later. Dinner is almost over and hilarity reigns. Leonard, Dinah and Parker have just taught Clio and Tate how to play the finger-snapping, handclapping game, Concentration. Plates pushed to one side, they're about to start a new round. Leonard's at the head of the table, with Tate on his left. Dinah's at the opposite end with Parker on her left and Clio on his left. They've changed into elegant nineteenth-century Chekhovian costumes. The encroaching trees and shrubs are starting to close in on them.

LEONARD *(Establishing the rhythm)*: Are you ready . . . ? If so . . . here we go . . . starting with . . . names of boats. *(Pause)* The *Titanic*!

TATE: The *Andrea Doria*!

DINAH: Um, um . . . the *Lusitania*! *(Placing her hand on his)* Parker . . . ?

PARKER: The *Normandy*! *(He empties his wine glass and slams it down for emphasis)*

CLIO: *Kon Tiki.*

LEONARD:	DINAH:	TATE:	PARKER:
Whoa!	Very good!	Nice!	*(Touches her shoulder, making a hissing sound)*

LEONARD *(Picking up speed)*: Um . . . the *Nina*!

TATE: The *Pinta*!

DINAH *(With a Spanish flourish)*: And the *Santa Maria*! Olé!

PARKER: The *Mayflower*! *(Reaches across Clio and helps himself to more wine)*

CLIO: The *Arabella,* John Winthrop's boat.

LEONARD:	DINAH:	TATE:	PARKER:
She's good.	My, my . . .	That's my girl!	*(Whistles)*

CLIO *(Helping herself to more stuffing)*: Mmmm, I can't stop eating this stuffing!

LEONARD *(Picking up speed, in a French accent)*: The *Île de France*!

TATE *(Likewise)*: The *De Grasse*!

DINAH: Um, um. . . . Help, I can't think!

ALL EXCEPT DINAH: You're out, you're out.

LEONARD: Go on, Park, it's your turn.

PARKER: The *Constitution. (He drains his glass)* Great wine!

DINAH: I've got it, I've got it, the *Intrepid*!

LEONARD *(To Parker)*: Glad you like it.

CLIO: The *Mauretania*! *(Helping herself to more)* Ohhh, this stuffing!

DINAH: The *Queen Mary*!

LEONARD: Dinah, you're out.

DINAH: The *Queen Elizabeth*!

LEONARD: The *Pequod*!

TATE: The *Pequod*?

DINAH: The *Q.E. II*!!

LEONARD: From *Moby Dick*.

TATE *(To Leonard, breaking the rhythm)*: I *know* where the *Pequod* comes from, I thought we were only naming real boats.

LEONARD *(To Tate)*: All boats, the more literary the better.

DINAH: The H.M.S. *Pinafore*!

TATE: Then why didn't you say so at the outset?

LEONARD: My apologies.

TATE: It *is* helpful to know the rules, you know.

LEONARD: You're right, you're right, I wasn't thinking.

TATE: Who knows what I might have come up with, I am an editor, after all.

CLIO *(Piling more stuffing on her plate)*: Ohhhh, what is it about this stuffing?

TATE: The *Antelope* from *Gulliver's Travels,* the *Patna* from *Lord Jim,* the *Nellie* from *Heart of Darkness . . .*

DINAH *(Starts singing)*:
I am the monarch of the sea,
The ruler of the Queen's Navee,
Whose praise Great Britain loudly chants.
And we are his sisters and his cousins and his aunts . . .
Come on, Parker, help me.

TATE *(To Leonard)*: So the sky's the limit? You're including boats from films and lyrics as well?

LEONARD: Everything, the works.

CLIO *(Joining Dinah)*:
And so do his sisters and his cousins and his aunts!
His sisters and his cousins,
Whom he reckons up by the dozens,
And his aunts!

PARKER *(Applauding Clio)*: Bravo, bravo! More wine?

CLIO *(Starting to get tipsy)*: Let 'er rip!

PARKER *(Filling Clio's glass and then his)*: I've got to hand it to you Handsome, this is terrific wine.

CLIO: And forget the stuffing!

LEONARD: Glad you like it, glad you like it.

PARKER: I haven't had this much fun in a dog's age.

Tate hands his glass to Parker to refill.

TATE: Party, party!

CLIO *(Running her hands down her bodice)*: And it's so great getting to wear these costumes!

PARKER *(To Dinah)*: God, I've missed you!

DINAH: Oh Parker . . .

CLIO: I feel like we're all in *The Cherry Orchard* or something.

PARKER: Remember the old days?

CLIO: I've played Varya three times.

DINAH: We used to dress up every night.

LEONARD: It's true.

PARKER: Every night. *(Returning Tate's filled glass)* Here you go.

CLIO: It's one of my favorite roles.

DINAH: Monday, Greek tragedy; Tuesday, Restoration comedy; Wednesday, Theater of the Absurd. . . . God, what happened?

PARKER: Good question.

LEONARD: Life.

PARKER: Shit.

TATE: Same difference.

PARKER: Hear, hear.

Silence.

CLIO *(Reciting as Varya)*: "I don't think anything will come of it for us. He is very busy, he hasn't any time for me—and doesn't notice me. God knows, it's painful for me to see him—"

DINAH *(To Parker)*: You went into movies, Leonard went crazy and I . . . who knows.

PARKER: Leonard's always been crazy.

LEONARD: I *have* always been crazy. I wonder why.

PARKER: Because you're an actor.

DINAH: Because he lost touch.

PARKER: All actors are crazy.

CLIO: Thanks a lot.

DINAH: He can't cope, he lives in his own world.

TATE:
Hey diddle diddle!
The cat and the fiddle,
The cow jumped over the moon . . .

LEONARD:
The little dog laughed
To see such sport
And the dish ran away with the spoon.
(To Tate) You're right, these little babies say it all.

Silence.

CLIO (*Reciting as Varya again*): "Everybody talks about our
marriage, everybody congratulates us, and the truth is, there's
nothing to it—it's all like a dream—*(Pause)* You have a brooch
looks like a bee."

PARKER (*Applauding Clio*): Nicely done.

TATE:

Hickety, pickety, my black hen,
She lays eggs for gentlemen.

Silence.

LEONARD (*To Parker, with sudden rage*): *You abandoned me, you
ingrate!*

DINAH: Leonard?

LEONARD: Once you left the theater, I never worked again.

PARKER: Hey, hey, you can't pin that on me.

LEONARD: No one wanted me. I was too old, too young, too
tall, too short, too real, too . . .

DINAH: That's not true, you were offered all kinds of roles.

LEONARD: Yeah, lousy ones.

PARKER: Work is work.

LEONARD: Bad plays, incompetent directors . . .

PARKER: You do what you have to do.

LEONARD: I have standards . . . unlike some people I know.

DINAH: Now, now . . .

LEONARD: Not all of us sell out.

PARKER: Opportunities present themselves, things change.

LEONARD: I don't change.

PARKER: Everything changes.

TATE:

Little Boy Blue,
Come blow your horn,
The sheep's in the meadow,
The cow's in the . . .

PARKER, LEONARD AND DINAH: *Will you shut up!*

TATE: Sorry, sorry . . .

Silence.

DINAH: Me, I'm designing six shows this season. It's insanity, but, hey, it puts food on the table.

TATE: And it was delicious.

DINAH: Thanks to you.

LEONARD *(To Parker)*: Why won't you cast me in a movie?

TATE *(To Dinah)*: Please.

LEONARD: Huh? *Huh?*!

PARKER: It's a different medium.

LEONARD: You mean, you only cast stars.

DINAH *(Suddenly clamps her hand down on her head)*: Ohhh, I just had the most massive déjà vu. Whoooooo . . .

CLIO: What causes those anyway?

DINAH: Ahhhhhhh . . .

TATE: They're small cerebral strokes, gentle prods to remind us that lunacy's just a heartbeat away.

LEONARD: Let's hear it for the crazy people! *(He rubs his finger up and down his lips)*

DINAH: Easy, honey, easy.

LEONARD *(Reaches a crescendo and stops)*: Ahhh, I needed that.

DINAH: The great thing about Leonard is he lets everything out. There's no holding back with him. Lucky dog.

LEONARD: It's one of my many gifts.

DINAH: It *is* a gift.

TATE: Indeed.

DINAH: I wish I had it.

LEONARD *(Bowing)*: Why, thank you.

Silence.

PARKER: Well, where were we?

Silence.

CLIO *(To Leonard)*: You just said the *Pequod*.

LEONARD: Right, right . . .

TATE *(Resumes the rhythm)*: The *African Queen*!

DINAH: The *Love Boat*!

LEONARD:	TATE:	PARKER:	CLIO:
Honey,	I thought	What's	No fair,
you're out!	she was out.	going on?	no fair.

PARKER *(Picking up speed)*: The *Caine* Mutiny!

CLIO: Mutiny on the *Bounty*!

LEONARD: The *Dixie Queen*!

DINAH: The Good Ship Lollipop!

ALL EXCEPT DINAH: YOU'RE OUT OF THE GAME!

DINAH: Ohhh, Noah's ark on you all!

LEONARD: Let's add marine figures of speech.

TATE: Um . . . *(Picking up speed)* Ship of state!

DINAH: Ship of Fools!

PARKER *(Eying Clio meaningfully)*: Shipshape!

CLIO *(Returning his gaze)*: Dreamboat.

PARKER *(Dropping the rhythm)*: Thar she blows!

CLIO *(With rising ardor)*: Batten down the hatches!

TATE *(To Clio)*: That's not a figure of speech.

DINAH: And it's not your turn.

PARKER *(Moving closer to her)*: Man overboard!

CLIO: S.O.S., S.O.S. . . .

PARKER: Coming about!

DINAH: Hey, hey . . .

CLIO: Shiver my timbers!

TATE: What's going on?

PARKER: Yo ho ho and a bottle of rum!

CLIO: Heigh ho, heigh ho, it's off to work we go.

PARKER: I'll huff and I'll puff and I'll blow your house down!

CLIO: Not by the hair of my chinny-chin-chin!

DINAH: Guys . . . ?!

TATE *(To Parker)*: It's not your turn!

PARKER *(To Clio)*: Rapunzel, Rapunzel, let down your hair!

CLIO: My, what big *teeth* you have!

PARKER *(Licking his chops)*: All the better to eat you with!

TATE AND DINAH: STOP THE GAME, STOP THE GAME!

Silence.

CLIO *(Collapsing against Parker)*: Ohhh, that was fun . . .
PARKER: You're really good.
CLIO: Well, you're not so bad yourself.

Dinah and Tate eye her angrily; she quickly straightens up.

DINAH: So . . . anyone want seconds on anything?

Silence.

DINAH *(She rises and starts to clear the table)*: Then on to the
salad!
TATE: There's more?
CLIO: I'm going to burst.
PARKER: What are you trying to do . . . ?
LEONARD: Hold on to your hats, you ain't seen nothing yet!
PARKER: Kill us?

Dinah exits to the kitchen.

PARKER:
(To Clio): So . . . how
often do you come up here?
Just weekends or . . . oh
sorry . . . sorry . . .

CLIO:
(To Parker): I can't
believe I finally met you!
(Hand over her heart)
Parker Bliss . . . !

Silence.

LEONARD:
(To Tate): So . . . how's
the renovation coming?
I see you're stripping the
paint right down to the . . .
sorry . . .

TATE:
(To Leonard): Tell me,
when was this house built?
I figure it was more or less
the same time as . . .
whoops . . .

Silence.

193

PARKER:
(To Clio): I was just
wondering how often
you . . .

CLIO:
*(To Parker, her hand
over heart)*: Boom boom,
boom boom, boom
boom . . .

Silence.

LEONARD:
(To Tate): That's got to
cost serious money. I also
notice you're repointing all
the . . .

TATE:
(To Leonard): I've
checked the records at
the County Clerk, but they
don't have anything before
1850 because of the . . .

Silence.

PARKER: . . . come here?

LEONARD: . . . chimneys!

TATE: . . . fire!

CLIO *(Placing his hand over her heart)*: Feel it.

PARKER *(Feeling it)*: Whoa!

CLIO: Boom boom, boom boom, boom boom!

Parker keeps his hand on her heart as Tate shoots them murderous looks.

CLIO *(Putting her hand over Parker's)*: Scary, huh?

DINAH *(Staggers in carrying a gigantic vat of salad. She pauses at the sight of Parker and Clio so intimately involved and drops the salad in front of them with a resounding thud)*: UUUUGH!

PARKER *(Pulling back in his chair)*: JESUS CHRIST . . .

CLIO: Look at the size of that bowl!

DINAH: I picked it fresh this morning.

CLIO: A person could take a bath in it.

DINAH: From inside the coat closet. It's like a greenhouse gone
   mad—mushrooms nesting in the mittens, avocados blooming
   in the galoshes, broccoli sprouting out the umbrellas . . .

LEONARD: She's exaggerating.

DINAH: A wave of vegetable lust is surging through the house, it keeps us awake at night. The pollinating and fertilizing, the germinating and foliating—you've never heard such a din . . . Green beans quickening, okra stiffening, zucchini swelling . . .

LEONARD: Dinah!

DINAH: Oh, the burgeoning and urgency of it all! *(Picks up a bottle of Wish Bone Italian salad dressing and reads the ingredients in a booming voice)* "Water, soybean oil, vinegar, salt, garlic, onion, sugar, red bell peppers, lemon juice . . ."

Dinah shakes the bottle so violently that everyone cowers in their seats.

LEONARD: Easy, easy!

DINAH *(Still shaking the bottle)*:   And then there's the roiling of the leafy things that wait! Swiss chard shuddering, spinach seething . . .

LEONARD: Don't mind her.

DINAH: Arugula unfurling on the chairs. Cabbage writhing, endive panting, hearts of palm ululating under the bed. *(She pours the dressing over the salad, splashing everyone in the process)*

LEONARD:	CLIO:	TATE:	PARKER:
Watch it!	Help!	Hey what's . . .	Look out!

DINAH: And don't forget the clamor of the ripening fruit. *(She starts tossing the salad)* The crooning of the cauliflower, the pleading of the chili peppers . . .

LEONARD: Dinah, Dinah . . .

DINAH *(Taking on their voices)*:   "Yoo hoo, here I am, behind the curtains."—"Pssst, over here, under the sink . . ."

PARKER *(Pushing away from the table)*:   Hey, hey . . .

DINAH: The entreaties of the tomatoes, the yodeling of the yams . . . "Look up, I'm inside the light fixture." "Open your eyes, you fool, I'm right under your nose!" *(She starts heaving spoonfuls of salad onto Parker)*

LEONARD *(Head in his hands)*:   Jesus God . . .

DINAH *(Burying Parker with rising abandon)*: The gasping and groaning, the clasping and moaning, you've never heard such carryings on. Cucumbers thrusting, carrots plunging . . .

PARKER *(Trying to ward her off)*: What do you think you're doing?

DINAH: Eggplants crying out for more . . .

LEONARD *(Grabbing her arms)*: Stop it, Dinah. Stop it!

DINAH: Tendrils snapping, seeds spattering, ruby red juices seeping through the floor . . .

LEONARD: *I'm begging you!*

PARKER *(Rises, pushing Dinah to the floor)*: GET A GRIP ON YOURSELF!

Dinah lands with a scream. There's an awful silence as Everyone stares at her.

TATE:

Mary, Mary, quite contrary,
How does your garden grow?
With silver bells and cockleshells
And pretty maids fornicating in a row.

Silence.

LEONARD *(Overcome)*: God, oh God, oh God . . .

TATE: Well, that was quite a . . .

Silence.

CLIO *(Rising)*: Excuse me, which way to the little girl's room?

LEONARD *(Pointing)*: Down the hall.

PARKER *(Rises, pulling back his chair)*: Madame . . .

CLIO *(To Parker)*: Don't get up.

Dinah gets up with a groan as Parker doffs an imaginary hat towards Clio.

DINAH *(To Parker, dusting herself off):* Ever the perfect gentleman.

Clio sashays down the hall. She throws Parker a backwards glance and disappears.
Silence.

LEONARD: Well . . .

DINAH: I'm sorry, I don't know what came over me.

LEONARD *(Softly):* Po-Po, Po-Po, I want Po-Po!

DINAH *(An an echo):* Po-Po.

TATE: The stick of the blind man invents a new darkness.

PARKER *(To Tate):* What was that again?

TATE: The stick of the blind man invents a new darkness.

PARKER: Nice, very nice.

TATE: I read it on a placard in a bus the other day.

LEONARD: My pope, my pip, my little pup . . .

DINAH: My dope, my dip, my little dup.

LEONARD: My yes, my own!

DINAH: My bless, my throne!

TATE *(Sotto voce to Parker):* Who's Po-Po?

PARKER: Their married daughter who lives in Tacoma. They're very close.

TATE: Ohh, I thought it was a pet.

PARKER: They like to shout out her name.

TATE: "Po-Po"?

PARKER: It's short for Phoebe.

LEONARD *(Mournful):* Po-Po, Po-Po, I want Po-Po!

PARKER: It's something they do. It's a way of staying in touch.

LEONARD *(Waving to Dinah):* Hi, Dine.

DINAH *(Waving back weakly):* Hi, Leonard.

LEONARD: How's it going?

DINAH: I don't like this anymore.

LEONARD: Me either.

DINAH: *No, I really don't like it!*

An awful silence.

TATE: Well, this has been quite an evening.

PARKER: I'll say.

TATE *(To Parker)*: You narrowly escaped death, we met our new neighbors, had a few laughs, got through the blight. I mean, *night*. That's the hard part.

DINAH: Tell me about it.

PARKER *(Raising his wineglass)*: To getting through the night.

Parker drinks. Tate joins him.

DINAH *(Starts clearing the table)*: So how about a little dessert?

PARKER: There's more?

TATE: I couldn't eat another bite.

PARKER: Me either.

LEONARD: When you come to our house for dinner, you *dine*, right Dine?

Parker groans at the play on words.

DINAH: You got it! And now for dessert—the pearl in the oyster, the ruby in the crown . . . *(She plunges into the kitchen)* Pumpkin pie, home grown, if you please!

| PARKER: | TATE: | LEONARD: |
| Dinah, Dinah . . . ! | Holy shit! | My favorite! |

DINAH: And . . . *(Returning, bearing them aloft)* Honey nougat meringue, compliments of Leonard's bees.

LEONARD: Let's hear it for the bees!

TATE: When it rains, it pours!

DINAH *(Setting them down with a thud)*: Gentlemen, go to it!

Clio emerges from the bathroom and slowly makes her way back to the dining room. Parker turns and sees her.

LEONARD *(Beaming at Dinah)*: Look at her! Have you ever seen anyone more beautiful? *(Pause)* Well, have you?

DINAH *(To Leonard, embarrassed)*: Honey . . . ?!

PARKER *(Quickly turning back to look at Dinah)*: Never!

TATE *(Reaching for the meringue)*: Well, maybe just a spoonful.
DINAH *(Handing each one a server)*: Dig in, dig in.
PARKER *(Rising from his seat)*: Excuse me, I'm afraid I'm going to have to use the facilities first . . .

Leonard attacks the pumpkin pie and Tate samples the meringue as Clio and Parker collide in the darkened hallway.

CLIO: Oh, hi.
PARKER: Hi.
CLIO *(Brushing against him)*: Sorry, I was just . . .
PARKER *(Suddenly grabs her in his arms)*: Ohhh, you wonder, you marvel, you shining girl . . . *(He pushes her against the wall)* You destroy me! I can't see, I can't walk, I'm in flames. *(He starts kissing her)*
CLIO: No, no don't, they'll see us.
PARKER *(All over her, barely audible)*: I wanted you the moment I saw you . . .
CLIO *(Starting to melt)*: Ohhhh . . . ohhhhhhh . . .
PARKER: Your face, your eyes, your skin, your voice. . . . Sweet Christ, I've never seen anything like you . . .
CLIO *(Returning his kisses)*: Ohhh . . . ohhhhhhh . . .

Even though they can't see them, Dinah and Tate hear every word and freeze in horror.

CLIO: Parker Bliss . . .
PARKER: Clio Hands . . .
TATE *(Rising from his seat)*: You son of a bitch . . .
LEONARD *(Wolfing down more pie)*: Ohhhh, this is great pie, Dine, *great* pie!

SCENE 2

Seconds later, Clio and Parker enter the room, shamefaced. No one moves.

DINAH *(To Parker)*: How could you . . . ?

TATE *(On his feet)*: I'm going to kill you!

LEONARD *(In ecstasies over the pie)*: Ohhhh, ohhhhh . . .

A ghastly silence as everyone looks at Leonard.

DINAH *(Embarrassed)*: Leonard . . . ?

TATE *(To Parker)*: That's my *wife,* you asshole!

LEONARD: It's so *moist! (He groans with pleasure)*

PARKER *(Returning to the table)*: Well, it's getting late.

CLIO *(Looking at her watch)*: It *is* getting late.

LEONARD: It's her specialty.

TATE *(Advancing towards Parker)*: Just who the hell do you think you are?

LEONARD *(Gobbling down more)*: Her *pièce de résistance . . .*

PARKER *(Backing away)*: Hey, hey . . .

CLIO *(Threading her arm through Tate's)*: Come on, we've got to get up early tomorrow.

TATE *(Shaking Clio off)*: I don't like guys manhandling my knife. *(He pushes Parker backwards)*

CLIO AND DINAH *(Correcting him)*: Wife.

PARKER: Take it easy.

TATE *(Pushing him harder)*: Make me!

LEONARD: Hey, what's going on?

DINAH *(To Leonard)*: Later, later . . .

PARKER: Are you threatening me?

TATE *(Pushing him harder)*: What does it look like?

CLIO *(Trying to pull Tate away)*: Toto!

TATE *(Violently pushing Clio away)*: Get your hands off me!

CLIO *(Massaging her wrist)*: Ow!

LEONARD *(Looking up from his pie)*: What happened?

PARKER *(To Tate)*: Don't push her.

TATE *(To Parker)*: What did you say?

LEONARD *(Louder, to Parker)*: What happened?

PARKER *(To Tate)*: I said: Don't. Push. Her.

DINAH *(To Leonard)*: Later, honey, later.

PARKER *(To Tate)*: What's the matter, do you have a hearing problem?

TATE: No, I have an asshole problem and it's you! *(He takes a swipe at Parker)*

CLIO: Tater, *please!*

DINAH *(Rushing between them)*: My costumes, my costumes!

CLIO: Oh God, the costumes! Careful, careful . . .

Tate and Parker quickly shed their costumes.

LEONARD: Will someone please tell me what's going on?

DINAH: Forget it Leonard, just crawl back in your hole.

CLIO: They're so beautiful, it would be terrible if they got damaged.

DINAH: It's like living with a dead person. You've gone, checked out, flown the coop . . .

PARKER *(Putting up his dukes)*: O.K., come to Papa . . .

LEONARD: "Flown the coop . . . ?"

TATE *(Dancing around him)*: You lowlife, you scum . . .

LEONARD *(To Dinah)*: What are you talking about?

DINAH: It's every man for himself.

PARKER *(Moving in on Tate)*: Pretentious wimp . . .

DINAH *(Rushing to shield Parker)*: *Don't touch him!*

CLIO *(Pulling at Tate)*: Stop it!

TATE *(Pushing Clio)*: Get away from me, bitch!

PARKER *(To Tate)*: Come on, hit me, hit me.

CLIO *(To Tate)*: Fuck you!

DINAH *(To Tate)*: I'm warning you. *(She bares her teeth and snarls)*

CLIO *(To Tate)*: Just, *fuck you!*

DINAH *(To Tate)*: Ass wipe!

CLIO *(To Tate)*: Dick head!

LEONARD *(To Tate)*: Scum bag!

TATE *(To Leonard)*: Just a minute here, he made a play for *my wife!*

DINAH: Butt wad!

CLIO: Shit face.

LEONARD: Jerk off!

TATE: Not that it's any great surprise, given her track record.

CLIO: What's that supposed to mean, "Given her track record?"

TATE:

Jack be nimble,
Jack be quick,
Jack jump over
The blind man's stick.

You'd better have quick reflexes, it's dark out there and very dangerous, in case you haven't noticed. There's a randomness at large, something wayward and unnatural.

LEONARD: One false move and you're done for. Kaput, fini . . . exit the king.

TATE: Mother Goose was no fool, she knew what was going on. Her rhymes are charms against disaster. Shout them out loud and often enough and you'll be safe. You should hear Clicks and I when the going gets rough. . . . She's very good. She makes up her own.

Silence.

PARKER: Well, I don't know about the rest of you, but I've got to get up early tomorrow. Patsy's got an opening at the Modern.

DINAH: Oh, don't go!

TATE *(To Parker)*: At the Modern?

PARKER: My wife's a sculptor.

CLIO *(To Tate)*: Come on, Pooks, time to go.

Tate doesn't move.

CLIO: *Pookie?!*

TATE: Right, right! *(To Parker)* You wouldn't be talking about Patsy Cincinnati, would you?

PARKER:	DINAH:	LEONARD:
You got it.	That's her.	The one and only.

CLIO AND TATE *(Stopping in their tracks)*: You're married to
Patsy Cincinnati?
PARKER: Whoops, I'd better put on some clothes here. *(He
grabs his shirt and starts putting it on)*
CLIO: Wow, Patsy Cincinnati!
TATE: She's major, her work's shown all over the world.
PARKER *(Thrusts out his arms and bows, revealing the bloodstain
again)*: Meet Mr. Patsy Cincinnati.

They all scream with horror.

DINAH: You can't wear that. Put the Chekhov shirt back on.

*Dinah helps Parker into the shirt. Clio and Tate look down at them-
selves and realize they're still in costume. They hastily start to change.*

CLIO: What's she like?
TATE: At the Tate, the Jeu de Paume, the Reina Sofia . . .
LEONARD: Tiny.
DINAH: And very feminine. You'd never know she was a sculp-
tor to look at her.
LEONARD: You can practically pick her up with one hand.
CLIO: You're kidding!
PARKER: I wouldn't try it, though.
TATE: The Castello de Rivoli, the Hara Museum, the Moderna
Museet . . .
PARKER *(To Tate)*: Well, well, don't we know the art scene.

Silence.

DINAH: She has wonderful hair.
PARKER: She does have wonderful hair.
DINAH *(Indicating on herself)*: Corkscrew curls out to here.
CLIO: Patsy Cincinnati. . . . Wow.
PARKER: I could drop off the face of the earth and she wouldn't
even notice.

DINAH AND LEONARD: *Parker?!*

PARKER: You know what she calls me these days? *Maestro!* She's forgotten my name. She leaves these messages on my answering machine—"Hi Maestro, it's me. How's Hollywood?" But hey, I can't complain, she's got a great eye. Look, she picked out this parka for me . . . *(Putting it on)* "I wanted to get you something warm," she said. "I don't want my Maestro shivering on the set." Well, you know Patsy and her circulation, the woman's got a perennial chill . . . *(Pause)* Let's just hope I don't run into anymore runaway mobile homes on my way back.

DINAH: Oh, don't leave.

LEONARD: Mobile homes, sinking homes, no one's safe.

TATE: You can say that again. Well, we ought to be heading along too. *(Hands Clio her coat)* Here you go, Clee.

CLIO *(Putting it on)*: Thanks Pooks. Luckily, we're right next door.

LEONARD: Well, you never know, crazed Enid Brill could always pop out of the bushes and mow you down.

DINAH *(Clinging to Parker's arm)*: Oh, stay a few minutes more.

TATE: Stop by the next time you pass the house, we could use a break.

CLIO *(Hugging Dinah)*: Yes, do, I feel so drawn to you. You're so *there.*

TATE *(Pulling Clio towards the door)*: Come on, Clue . . .

CLIO *(To Dinah)*: If I don't call you, you call me, O.K.? It can get pretty lonely around here, in case you haven't noticed. I've been abandonéd.

LEONARD *(Impressed with her accenting)*: My, my!

CLIO: Stranded in the middle of nowhere.

TATE *(Putting his arm around her)*: But with me.

CLIO: I'm never with you. You're either working or locked up with the painters and carpenters. When I walk in a room you don't even see me. I wave and it's like no one is there. Well, someday you'll take me in and when that happens . . . *(Getting weepy)* Oh my . . . *(Recovering)* Once we get the place fixed up we'll just be here weekends and during the summer, but Tate insists we live here while the work's being done. You know, *to*

keep an eye on things. He's temporarily moved his office up here.
I've never renovated a house before, so I'm not that much help.
I look at wallpaper, pick out paint and talk to the contractor—
that is, when he shows up. Which is hardly ever.

TATE *(Hands over his ears)*: Don't . . .

CLIO: He's impossible. He's also the fattest man I've ever seen.
And the hairiest. He has a full beard and is covered with fur,
thick brown fur. He looks like a woolly mammoth.

LEONARD AND DINAH: Frank Flood.

CLIO AND TATE: Frank Flood.

DINAH: She's right, he *does* look like a woolly mammoth!

PARKER: Woolly mammoths. . . . I love woolly mammoths!

LEONARD: He's the best, the best.

TATE: But try getting him to make an appearance.

CLIO: I'm quite fond of him, actually. He's one of the few
people I see. I have fantasies of leaping on his shoulders and
galloping back to the dawn of time. Just him and me and the
saber tooth tigers. *(Pause)* Thank God I've got a film this
spring.

*Clio reaches into her bag, pulls out a scrap of paper and quickly
scribbles down her phone number.*

TATE *(Shaking hands with Dinah and Leonard)*: We had a great
time. Good food, lively conversation . . .

CLIO *(To Dinah)*: Now call me.

DINAH: I will.

CLIO: Don't forget.

DINAH: Wait a minute, let me give you some of Leonard's
honey. *(She starts rummaging through a drawer)*

PARKER *(Shaking hands with Clio)*: It was a pleasure.

CLIO: Likewise. *(She slips Parker the piece of paper with her
phone number on it)*

DINAH *(Handing Tate several jars of honey)*: Here you go.

PARKER *(Glancing at it)*: Why, thank you.

TATE: Much obliged. *(Pulling her towards the door)* O.K., Coco,
time to go home.

LEONARD: I'll get the door. *(He opens it)*

The wind howls louder than ever.

LEONARD: Fucking wind!
TATE: Thanks again. Next time you must come to our house. *(He pulls Clio after him)*
CLIO *(Waving)*: Good night, good night . . .
DINAH: Quick, shut the door.
LEONARD *(Slams the door behind them)*: Son of a bitch!
DINAH: Well, that was quite a . . .

Silence.

LEONARD *(To Parker)*: Come on, take off your coat and stay awhile.
PARKER *(Zipping up his parka)*: I've really got to go.
DINAH *(Hanging on him)*: Stay, stay!
PARKER: I can't.
LEONARD: We haven't begun to catch up.
DINAH: Spend the night.
PARKER: I *can't*!
LEONARD: Please?
DINAH: Pretty please?
PARKER *(Opening his arms to Leonard)*: Come here, you lunatic.

Leonard rushes into them.

PARKER *(Lifting him off the ground)*: Ughhh!
LEONARD: Come on, stay! You can sleep in Po-Po's room.
PARKER *(Lets him go and opens his arms to Dinah)*: Hey, Threads . . .
DINAH *(Rushing into them)*: Oh Parker, Parker . . . !
PARKER: That's my girl.
DINAH *(Clinging to him)*: Don't go!
PARKER *(Pulling away)*: I've got to, Patsy's waiting.
DINAH: Stay, I'm begging you!

PARKER (*Putting an arm around each of them*): Guys, it was great, just like the old days. I forgot how much fun you were. I don't have friends like you anymore. Funny how things change.

LEONARD: Hilarious.

PARKER: Here I am this big movie director and I don't have any real friends.

LEONARD: My heart is breaking.

PARKER: And then there's the work, which is a whole other kettle of fish. Or is it worms? It sure ain't Shakespeare. Oh well, we do our best. Right?

LEONARD: *Do* we?

PARKER (*Heading out the door*): O.K., I've got to go.

DINAH (*Reaching for him*): Come back!

PARKER: I'll call you in a couple of days, I promise. (*And he's gone*)

DINAH (*Running out the door after him*): Don't leave me . . .

LEONARD: Easy, Dine, easy . . .

DINAH: Don't leave me!

LEONARD (*Pulling her back inside*): Where are you going?

DINAH: Come back!

LEONARD (*Slamming the door shut*): It's cold out there.

DINAH (*Getting weepy*): He left, he left . . .

LEONARD: Well, that's Parker for you. Selfish son of a bitch.

DINAH (*Throwing herself face down on the sofa*): Oh, Leonard. . . .

Silence.

LEONARD: So, what did you think of the evening?

DINAH: It was a disaster.

LEONARD: It *was* a disaster, wasn't it?

DINAH: Total.

LEONARD: What did you think of our new neighbors?

DINAH: I couldn't stand them.

LEONARD: She was very taken with you.

DINAH: I'd say Parker was the one she was taken with.

LEONARD (*With disgust*): Parker!

Dinah sighs. Silence.

LEONARD: You know, you looked really beautiful tonight.
DINAH: Please!
LEONARD: No, you did.
DINAH: Not next to her.
LEONARD: I'd take you over her any day, no contest.
DINAH: Well, Parker seemed to like her.
LEONARD: Parker . . .

Silence.

LEONARD: Well, that was quite some performance with the salad.
DINAH: Salad . . . ?
LEONARD: Talk about throwing yourself at someone.
DINAH: I don't know what came over me.
LEONARD: How do you think it made me feel?
DINAH: I couldn't stop myself.
LEONARD *(Covering his ears)*: I don't want to hear.
DINAH: Once I started, I just . . .
LEONARD: I said, *I don't want to hear!*
DINAH: Sorry, sorry . . .
LEONARD: Give a guy a break.

Silence.

DINAH *(Rising)*: God, look at the place. It looks as if a bomb went off. *(She starts putting the costumes away)*
LEONARD: Something did happen between you. It was during the production of *Cyrano.* There was a real charge between you. Hello . . . ? You there in the Chekhov outfit. I'm right, aren't I? You can tell me, it was almost ten years ago.
DINAH: Twelve.
LEONARD: Whatever.
DINAH: Twelve and a half, to be exact.

TINA HOWE

LEONARD: Parker's a very charismatic guy, look what happened to Whoosis tonight.

DINAH: *Clio Clio! Think Cleopatra, for Christ's sake! It's not that hard a name!*

LEONARD: You don't have to yell.

DINAH *(Starts clearing the table)*: I mean, after awhile . . .

LEONARD: She succumbed while her husband was in the room, at least you were more discreet. Come on, tell me, I can take it.

DINAH *(Sings, carrying the dishes into the kitchen)*:
Someone's in the kitchen with Dinah
Someone's in the kitchen I know, ow, ow, ow . . .
Someone's in the kitchen with Dinah,
Strumming on the old banjo . . .

LEONARD: What happened?

DINAH *(Returning)*:
They're strumming fee, fi, fiddly-i-o;
Fee, fie fiddly-i-o;
Fee, fie, fiddly-i-ooooo . . .
Strumming on the old banjo.

LEONARD: Well . . . ?

DINAH: Give it up, Dinah, just *give it up.*

LEONARD: I'm waiting.

DINAH: O.K. . . . We were in your dressing room going over some costume changes after the show one night. The theater was empty, it was just Parker and me in a sea of plumes and doublets, and suddenly he's all over me, his hands, his mouth, his tongue, anything that protrudes. . . . And he's murmuring, "Ohhhh, you wonder, you marvel, you shining girl. You destroy me! I can't see, I can't walk, I'm in flames. . . . Your face, your eyes, your skin, your voice . . . "

LEONARD: Why does that sound so familiar?

DINAH: Because he just said it to Clio five minutes ago. The only difference is she gave in and I didn't.

LEONARD: What did you say?

DINAH: I said, *she gave in and I didn't!* What's the matter, are you deaf now too?

LEONARD: Nothing happened?

DINAH: I guess I showed them. Oh yes, I showed them good!

LEONARD: *Nothing happened?*

DINAH: That's right, rub it in.

LEONARD: Nothing happened.

DINAH: And one more time. *(Waving her arms like a conductor, she mouths "Nothing happened")* It's a shocker, but there you are.

LEONARD: I don't know what to say.

DINAH: The joke's on me. Everyone assumed it was a fait accompli, so it wouldn't have made any difference. Good old Dinah, ever the dutiful wife. *(Imitating herself)* "It's not right, Leonard would never get over it, he's bound to find out, I know him. He'll see it in my eyes, he'll smell it in my hair, nothing gets past him when it comes to me."

LEONARD: You were faithful.

DINAH: If you can call it that. I wanted him, I just couldn't go through with it. Don't ask me why, I've been trying to figure it out for the past eighty years. No, ask, ask . . . on second thought, you'd better not, it's too humiliating.

LEONARD: You didn't do it, you didn't do it!

DINAH: I lacked courage, I wasn't up to it. It's pathetic.

LEONARD: And all this time I thought . . . *(Folding her in his arms)* Oh baby, baby . . .

DINAH: I wanted him.

LEONARD: You didn't do it.

DINAH: I wanted him.

LEONARD: It's all right.

DINAH: Oh Leonard . . .

LEONARD: Let it out . . .

DINAH: You're not listening to me. *(She starts to cry)* I said, *I wanted him, I wanted him, I wanted him, I wanted him . . .*

LEONARD: I know, I've always known. I've just been lying low. But you . . . how you held your ground all these years. . . . It takes my breath away. You don't lack courage, you can't contain it! You're like the cauliflower under our bed, fierce and tenacious . . .

DINAH: Oh Leonard . . .

They look at each other and slowly embrace. The wind starts to howl.

LEONARD: Fucking wind!

DINAH: I can't take it anymore! *(She rushes to the front door and flings it open, facing the wind)* HEY, YOU OUT THERE, LET UP ALREADY! SHOW A LITTLE RESPECT FOR ONCE. WE'VE GOT SOME SERIOUS CATASTROPHES ON OUR HANDS!

The wind howls louder.

DINAH: A BREAKDOWN HERE, A LOSS OF NERVE THERE, A MAJOR IMBALANCE IN THE ORDER OF THINGS . . . *(Pause)* SAVINGS GONE . . .

LEONARD *(Joining her)*: A BACKED-UP SEPTIC TANK . . .

DINAH: TWENTY DOLLARS IN THE CHECKING ACCOUNT . . .

LEONARD: CORRODING WATER PIPES . . .

DINAH: TEN MORE YEARS ON THE MORTGAGE . . .

LEONARD: A LEAKING ROOF . . .

DINAH: WE'D APPRECIATE SOME PEACE AND QUIET, IF YOU DON'T MIND. *(Dinah retreats a few steps)*

LEONARD: Bats in the attic . . .

DINAH: Mice in the basement . . .

LEONARD: Swallows in the kitchen . . .

DINAH: Eagles in the pantry . . .

LEONARD *(To Dinah)*: *Eagles* in the pantry?

DINAH *(Heading back into the wind, yelling with new fury)*: I'M NOT ASKING, I'M TELLING YOU. IT'S TIME FOR A CHANGE!

Leonard joins her, pulling her close. They hold their ground against the gale which finally starts to subside.

The curtain slowly falls.